CONSTRUCTIVE
AWARENESS

CONSTRUCTIVE AWARENESS

ALEXANDER TECHNIQUE
AND
THE SPIRITUAL QUEST

DANIEL McGOWAN

PUBLISHED FOR THE PAUL BRUNTON
PHILOSOPHIC FOUNDATION BY

LARSON PUBLICATIONS

International Standard Book Number: 0-943914-85-X
Library of Congress Catalog Card Number: 97-74021

Published for the Paul Brunton Philosophic Foundation by
Larson Publications
4936 NYS Route 414
Burdett, NY 14818 USA

04 03 02 01 00 99 98 97

10 9 8 7 6 5 4 3 2 1

to
The Shining One

ACKNOWLEDGEMENTS

Deepest gratitude to Randy and Amy Cash, Gunda Fielden, and Gerda and Thoms Törring for their contribution to the production of this text.

CONTENTS

What philosophy seeks—and what most
"systems" do not—is an all-around understanding
and development, and an equilibrium between the
body and the higher individuality.

Paul Brunton

INTRODUCTION

THE PRINCIPLES and procedures of F.M. Alexander are crucially needed at present. This book is no literary gem. The thoughts contained in it did not come easily. Neither did the process of transferring them from mind to paper. These words have been written after some years of life experience and study, and are the result of much heart-searching. The reader who is unable to consider them with an open mind, free from preconceived ideas, should stop now. The reader who needs scintillating statements and flowing lines should also read no further. I make no claims to being a writer.

Certain statements herein are made from two standpoints, one being the philosophic, the other the practical. In writing about the human being, the self, correct philosophical language is too boring and cumbersome. For example, from the philosophic standpoint, one would have to refer repeatedly to the body as "the part of the mind known as the body." Also, the term "psycho-physical unity" is inadequate, but necessary, to convey the idea that there is no difference between the mind and the body; they are both made of mental "stuff."

We require a totally new language to discuss the self, because our way of referring to it is historically based on the common belief that the body is a material object. This is a very powerful, habitual assumption.

The reader will find the repetition in these pages either a pleasant feature or an unnecessary irritation. I have consciously chosen to repeat certain statements because, in my experience of teaching constructive awareness, I have observed that it is often necessary to tell a person not only once or twice, but three times and more when attempting to convey difficult ideas.

A particular difficulty for me lies in attempting to define "spirituality." I see it as the human being's desire to cultivate the finer feelings of love, humility, calmness, confidence, courage, compassion, altruism, and kindness in his or her interaction with other people, other creatures, during the course of a lifetime on this planet. I also see, as a necessary part of spirituality, that these finer feelings should be extended to—nay, should begin with being directed to—the billions of intelligent living beings that constitute my own body. This is the foundation of human love.

The other aspect of "spirituality" I am not so sure of; that is, the life of the spirit beyond the veil, on the other side, after death, call it what you will. I am sure, though, of the survival, after death, of the essence of the individual in this spiritual sphere, or more correctly, mental sphere.

Constructive Awareness

Alexander Technique and the Spiritual Quest

With most people the reaction to their environment and to events is mainly impulsive and
mostly uncontrolled. So the first step for them
is to become conscious of what they are doing,
the second being to refuse to do it when reflection and wisdom dictate a better course.
All this implies a taking hold of the self and a
disciplining of its mechanism—body, feelings,
and thoughts. It leads to using the self with
awareness and functioning in it with efficiency.

Paul Brunton

1

WHAT BODY?

THIS BOOK is for the seeker, the person on a path of spiritual inquiry that begins with the self's environment, the world, and ends with its center, the Self. At some point in the lives of thinking persons, questions about the nature of the world, the body, and the mind come up; they trouble such people persistently enough to make them dig deeper until they arrive at the conclusion that knowledge of the Self is fundamental to all other knowledge. The seeker, then, is driven by the need to find answers to the following questions.

1. What is the mind?
2. What is the body?
3. What is the world?
4. What is the source of happiness?
5. What am I?

It is not my purpose to answer these questions, but first to throw some light on the interaction of the mind with the body and the world. Then I hope to show how a better understanding of this interaction will bring real knowledge of one aspect of that Self which is the common basis of all three. This aspect is the Self's *active* phase as it deals with the *form* side of life. Such an understanding of this interaction in our everyday lives and activities, although perhaps not the source of happiness, can certainly bring deep joy and satisfaction on our journey through this incarnation.

The process of constructive awareness outlined in this book will, if carefully considered, help the seeker to come nearer to finding the answer to that most difficult of all questions, "What am I?"

The relationships of the mind to the body and the body to the world are still greatly misunderstood by the modern person. In these days of more open-mindedness in the West to Eastern philosophy and religion, the unity of the mind-body-world complex is accepted intellectually by many seekers. But this acceptance gives them very little that is practical and tangible with which to work, in order to realize this unity as a vital fact of our existence.

At the mundane, everyday level of our lives, separateness still reigns. On the one hand, we think abstractly in our heads. On the other, we perform our daily tasks physically with the body as it is affected by, or does things to, its environment which is "out there."

Let us consider the mind-body relationship. To do this we must examine our beliefs about what the mind is and what the body is. The common materialistic view is that the brain is the seat of consciousness which somehow gives rise to the fundamental thought of the "I," the ego, and all other thoughts which spring from this root. It is assumed that consciousness is a result of molecular disturbances in the brain. A study of the doctrine of mentalism, however, begins to cast a few doubts about the validity of this simplistic assumption. Staying with the materialistic view: If the brain is the seat of consciousness, then the "mental" activity which occurs in it would be the subjective element in us; everything outside the brain—that is, the rest of the body and the world—would be objective.

Thus we face a queer situation where this objective, material body sends reports to the brain via the senses of sight, hearing, taste, touch, smell, and proprioception, which are also regarded as subjective. The confusion which reigns about this situation is apparent when we consider how often we habitually refer to the body as the self, the "I." The mentalness of the "I" is here forgotten. The confusion increases because this "I," this body, is habitually regarded as a material object—a special, intimate one, yes, but material nonetheless. Extending this reasoning—or, more correctly, this confusion—to the mind-body-world complex, all things which stand outside the body are commonly believed to be material phenomena.

The mentalistic view is fundamentally different. Although the subject is too vast to enter into deeply in this little book, a few of its key points will be given, both in relation to the mind-body complex and the mind-body-world complex.

Mentalism states simply that although all objects in the world, even in the universe, stand outside the body, they do not stand outside the mind. The mind is not contained by or confined inside the head. It simply is. It is something given. Where it begins and ends, nobody knows. It is that miraculous essence of us which thinks and which knows. To talk of things being inside or outside the mind is pointless. In the end, all is mental. This knowledge, however, does not alter the powerful feeling that the faculties of sight, hearing, taste, touch, smell, and proprioception are subjective and that all things outside the body are objective.

The relativity of subjective faculties and objective phenomena constitutes human experience in the waking state. Without the former we cannot know the latter. In other words no "material" object can be known without presupposing a mind to know it. This inexorable relativity reveals that what we see and know as the "outside" world is directly connected with our organs of perception and knowledge. What we perceive has neither more nor less reality than our perception. The material world—including the body—of our everyday experience is consequently seen to possess a different reality than that which we have unconsciously given it. The world and all things in it are definitely not what they appear to be. The world is not filled with a host of material objects that exist in their own right and have the identical forms that our perception gives them. Things cannot stand alone in isolation; they must be known by some mind. We cannot assume that objects which stand outside the body possess any self-identical extension at all independently of our faculties of perception. In short, our perception of the world—including the body—is the world.

From mentalism, then, we learn that the body is a state of mind; this is the philosophic standpoint. This knowledge, however, does not make the feeling of the body as a material object any less powerful. Neither does it diminish the pains and pleasures which the body experiences. Through sensation it brings us pain or pleasure, and its condition determines the quality of our lives.

The body, unfortunately, tends to be forgotten, a little neglected, and certainly misused by almost everyone, including spiritual seekers. Sometimes it is particularly misused by spiritual seekers, who tend to divide their attention between two extremes: the first being the environment and the second the higher Self during meditation. The first state is that of extroverted attention as we deal with the practical affairs of our everyday lives. The second is one of introverted concentration as we attempt to still the mind.

The medium through which we perform in these two extreme states is the body, that wonderful instrument of which most of us know very little, as a mechanism. Yet we endeavor to make it be still and quiet during meditation periods or ask it to perform actively during our everyday existence.

We expect this body to perform its daily tasks smoothly and easily, and all goes well if it does so. If it functions well and gives us no trouble, we tend to ignore it. But when it starts to complain through discomfort and pain, we are forced to take note of its existence and needs. If the body continues to complain and be ill, we are obliged, through pain, to be even more aware of it. We may try all sorts of remedies to improve its condition, but very often the body cannot return to a really healthy state: The activities we enjoy in life, as well as "important" things like our jobs, then pale into insignificance in comparison to the need to be free of pain and discomfort.

Philosophy urges us to learn to live consciously in the moment.

Illness, however, *forces* this hard lesson upon us. When we have it, we don't care much about what will happen next week or next year, etc., nor do we care to remember events of the past. The desirable state is that of existing in a pain-free body, or at least less painful body. How does one achieve this?

Let us return to the consideration of the body as a mechanism and make a bold statement: The most fundamental reason for physical ills in the modern person is misuse of our *thinking*; this results in misuse of the body in all areas of human activity, but chiefly in the significant areas of our so-called mundane, everyday activities such as walking, sitting, standing, eating, bending, lifting, thinking, cleaning ourselves, and so on. The list is endless. The vast majority of us have failed to consider that the quality of our movements in these "unimportant" activities has a tremendous bearing on the quality of our lives in general. The idea that the body can perform these trivial acts easily is a fallacy. The tremendous importance of good use of the body is usually missed.

What is meant by the terms "misuse" and "good use" of the body? The former means that we use the body in ways for which it was not designed. This includes ways which use excessive muscle tension when doing something, using muscles that are not needed for a particular task, distorting the neck, back, shoulders, hips, etc., and interfering harmfully with the breathing mechanism. From misuse, muscles become stiff and shortened and the body in general decreases in stature. This compressed state also interferes adversely with the functioning of the vital organs in the torso, because they are forced to function in cramped conditions. This leads to all kinds of maladies, such as poor breathing, sluggish circulation, inadequate assimilation and elimination of food, and so on.

A good example of using excessive muscular effort is that of lifting an empty kettle which one assumed was full of water and raising it too high before realizing it is empty. This also means that we have adopted an unnecessary "postural set" in the muscles in order to lift the kettle. This postural set is subconscious; it occurs beneath our awareness and also points significantly to the fact that we habitually perform thousands of everyday tasks with excessive, inappropriate effort. Small wonder we become tired and listless.

Good use, in contrast, comes from a proper consideration of the body as a mechanism. This allows the body to perform freely and easily, with a strong back and suitable effort for each task, with poise and balance and with appropriate muscle tension. One result of balanced use of the body is economy of movement, a saving of energy which allows us to keep our vitality. Good use does not mean relaxation as it is generally understood, because that leads to flaccidity in the muscles and, in the modern person, usually means an undesirable state of collapse. Balanced muscle tension throughout the body is the ideal condition.

The body's role in the present incarnation is vital and its implications for the seeker should be apparent. Awareness of the body arises on waking from deep sleep, at the same time as our awareness of the environment. The body and the world ultimately are one. It is impossible to think of yourself being physically anywhere in the world or even the universe without being in an environment. Unity is simply a fact of life!

If, on our spiritual quest, we are mainly ignorant of the most immediate, vital part of our environment, namely the body, and if we do not give it its proper place and treat it with love, respect, and reverence, we will be hampered in our attempts to lead a more spiritual life. We are no less spiritual for giving proper regard to the body. Constructive awareness of it during the here-and-now of our lives makes much more sense than relegating it to an inferior position while we try to pierce the veil of the beyond in our efforts to understand higher states like "spirit" and "mind."

Any attempts to pursue a spiritual quest must include due consideration of the body, if not sooner then undoubtedly later. Increased knowledge of spirit, mind, and body should occur simultaneously, not one after the other, if a balanced existence is to be achieved. As stated earlier, being in the moment, being aware of the quality of our physical, everyday acts in a pain-free body is a highly desirable state to be in. It is also a necessary state, which can be used as a springboard for our spiritual aspirations.

Although the questions "What is the world?" and "What is the body?" have not here been approached directly, the fact of their unity has been emphasized together with the quality of life which we can cultivate for ourselves through constructive awareness of the body. We can now consider this constructive awareness in the next chapter.

It comes to this: constructive awareness should be used in the staggering repetition of the everyday acts of our life. A therapy it is not, a "method" it is not. It is the natural function of the conscious mind. The IS is not an ism.

Anonymous

2

CONSTRUCTIVE AWARENESS

AS EXPLAINED in the previous chapter, misuse of our thinking, resulting in misuse of the body, is a present-day malady. The modern person is a victim of generations of misuse caused by artificial living conditions in civilization. These artificial, stressful conditions cause taut necks, rounded backs, stiff joints, inadequate breathing, stretched nerves, all kinds of neuroses, worried minds, and so on. Such is our unawareness of ourselves that these states can come to feel "normal," to be "us." In other words, we develop a habitual, devitalized way of being and doing. Our habits are us. This devitalized condition is usually considered to be an unavoidable part of life, something that is inevitable as we grow older, and we usually blame something or someone else for our situation.

Consider, though, how much of this way of being is of our own making, is our own responsibility. The environmental conditions into which one is born, or lives in, cannot be excluded from this consideration; indeed, extremely adverse situations play a large part in shaping our lives. If such conditions, however, are within reasonable limits, they can be ignored for the purpose of this illustration.

One of the strongest habits that we develop from early childhood is that of "end-gaining." This means a constant striving to get to the end of any task that we perform, without proper consideration of the co-ordinated "means" we should employ to gain the desired end. Education is geared to end-gaining. Children are encouraged to produce a good result at school or college without proper consideration of the "how" of achieving it without losing their psycho-physical equilibrium. This is true of so-called mental as well as physical activities.

The best way to illustrate the difference between "end-gaining" and "means" is to give a simple example, such as the act of picking up an object from the floor. The vast majority of us react to the stimulus of the object falling on the floor by bending the torso forward at the lumbar spine and keeping the knees straight as we reach down with the hand. This movement continues until the knees have to be reluctantly bent to allow the hand to reach and grasp the object. The return journey usually starts with placing the hands on the knees and pushing up with the arms because the back is not strong enough to perform this task easily. The breath is held throughout this activity—except for when a tired grunt of effort is forced from the body. This habitual way of bending the back can be extremely detrimental to the welfare of the lumbar spine. If done too often, it can lead to damage to the intervertebral discs in the form of distortions and even prolapse.

If you ask a person to describe in detail what she actually did with the different parts of the body in lifting up the object, she would be unable to do so. This is because the co-ordinated "means" of performing the act are of little interest to her and occur beneath her awareness. She will have no more than a vague, hazy idea of the "how" of her doing. This is classic, habitual "end-gaining."

A more mechanically appropriate way of bending to the floor is to allow the back to remain "straight" and to bend the knee and hip joints, as young children do.

The above explanation, however, does not go far enough as it gives the impression that we can change *directly* one method of doing something for a better one. This example is given simply to point out that a superior, mechanically appropriate method exists; but if this were as far as it goes, we would be dealing with nothing more than physical culture. The *indirect* process of constructive awareness is much more than mere physical culture; to learn it, we ought to begin to use our minds and consider the "how" of performing our everyday activities. We can learn how to constructively "think in activity," how to attend to the co-ordinated "means" of doing something, no matter how trivial.

The first method of bending in the above example is a misuse of the body mechanism; it is not designed to do this. Numerous other examples could be given of the inappropriate, detrimental habits of use of the psycho-physical self.

Physical habits cause mental habits and vice versa. Sects, cults, and groups which recognize, and which attempt to utilize, the power of the mind over the body are out of truth, and so out of balance, to the extent that they fail to appreciate equally the power of the body over the mind. The way to change bad physical and mental habits is by inhibiting them. Inhibition in the sense meant here is the very basis of change. But before we can consider it, we must look first at the power of habit.

Note: The reader is asked to be aware that although this chapter on "Constructive Awareness" is small, its importance should not be underestimated. A longer chapter is not necessary, as constructive awareness is the recurrent theme of the whole book.

The faulty use of the body is a consequence of
the failure to bring both awareness and reflection
into it. This is to be guarded against because
civilized living has substituted artificial habits
for the natural ones of the primitive.

Paul Brunton

Psycho-physical equilibrium cannot be achieved
unless the habits which obstruct it are changed.

Anonymous

3

THE POWER OF HABIT

OBSERVE someone whom you know well doing something, like sitting down in an easy chair. You will notice that she performs this act more or less in the same way every time. The act occurs as follows.

As the person approaches the chair, the body shortens in stature as a muscular set is adopted in anticipation of sitting down. The back is then bent further, followed reluctantly by the knees until the bum makes heavy contact with the seat of the chair. The torso then leans back onto the back of the chair, which is usually "built for comfort" and shaped to cater for such a slumped back. One leg is crossed over the other, the arms are folded over the abdomen, and the head is poked forward as she stares at the TV. In other words, during the act of sitting, the integrity of the primary unifying reflex mechanism in the body is interfered with. This reflex mechanism is the *head-neck-back relationship*, which is upset by unduly stiffening the neck muscles, causing them to shorten, thus pulling the head back and down into the shoulders. In addition, the back is shortened and narrowed, and the breath is shallow or stopped completely. This harmful position is maintained subconsciously for quite some time as she is absorbed in the TV program.

This mechanically inappropriate method of sitting down and remaining seated is a typically strong habit for the vast majority of us. We are unaware of what we actually do with the body on the journey from standing to sitting.

One does not generally have a choice of how to sit down. This is because, after receiving the stimulus of deciding to do so, each attitude of the body which is adopted, step by step, during each millimeter of the journey, is determined by the step before. In other words, each minute step is the habitual straitjacket for the next one. This means that the person is a slave to habits which are very powerful because they have been repeated thousands of times during a lifetime.

Why is this so? The answer is that the brain is locked in a groove, a thought-groove. As soon as one receives the stimulus to sit down, the same neurons are sparked into activity in the brain, the same messages are sent down the same channels, and the muscles react in the same old way. This is the physiological fact of a habit.

Another interesting aspect of a habit is seen in the person who stoops badly while standing. If you point out to her that she stoops, she will immediately pull herself up to an erect situation and attempt to improve her way of standing directly. Within a short time, she will be back to the old habit of stooping, because it is so powerful and its influence irresistible. The person who stoops all the time actually believes that the reason she does so is simply that she is omitting or forgetting to stand upright in a strong, graceful manner. *This belief is a delusion.*

As stated earlier, this habit of stooping interferes with the head-neck-back relationship and denies that relationship its proper function as the primary unifying reflex mechanism in the body. *The quality of this relationship determines the quality of the functioning and movement of all other parts of the organism.*

We usually think of people as having good or bad posture, but we do not consider that our postural state determines the quality of our movements. In other words, posture is basic to movement. The energy mobilized in posture is released into a pattern of activity that can be seen as each individual's unique way of moving. In posture, one should be as truly active as in movement. If I stoop all the time, for example, this will mean that my posture is fixed or stiff; my movements will be of similar poor quality. If, however, the head-neck-back relationship is allowed its proper, balanced function, I will be as fluent or mobile in posture as I am in movement.

The poise of the head, the freedom of the neck, the posture of the spine, and the function of the breath determine every attitude of the whole organism. If these functions are harmfully interfered with through poor posture and movement, through habitual misuse, we will go through life performing beneath our best. This means not only performing badly the activities we love to participate in—music, dance, sport, hobbies, and so on—but also the more important ones such as walking, sitting, standing, eating, cleaning ourselves, bending, lifting, and writing. I refer to the latter activities as "more important" because they are tasks we usually consider too trivial to give our attention. They are, however, acts we have to perform thousands of times in our daily lives; this appalling repetition blinds us to their vital significance. To improve the quality of our living in general, we should become conscious of the quality of our movements in these everyday activities.

How does one do this? Adopting the process of constructive awareness will restore the integrity of the head-neck-back relationship, which in turn will restore the body to a state of co-ordination and balance. In other words, we should change our harmful, habitual use of the organism by first learning to *stop* or *inhibit* our old habitual way of being; then, through our wonderful power of thinking, we can consciously direct the body in a physically or mechanically appropriate manner that will lead to balance, ease of movement, co-ordination and the proper functioning of the vital organs.

The ability to *inhibit* is fundamental to the process of change and will be explained together with *direction* in the next chapter. If we do not learn to inhibit or stop our old, harmful habits, we will be unable to direct ourselves to adopt new, beneficial ones.

The intelligence in the deeper human mind manufactures the bodily organs it requires for experience or development. In this way it has built the entire body itself.

Paul Brunton

4

INHIBITION AND DIRECTION

THE VAST majority of us believe that if we are asked to perform an act in a new, unfamiliar manner, we can simply do it. This belief is a fallacy. To perform an act in a familiar way is a simple matter, but to do so in a new way involves experiences for which we must take a step into the unknown. In my experience of teaching constructive awareness, I have very rarely found anyone, no matter how intellectual, who could overcome the irresistible power of their habitual behavior and easily switch to this new, unknown way. Why?

Let us consider again the apparently simple act of sitting in a chair. As described earlier, the person will sit down in a familiar, habitual manner which involves misusing the body as a mechanism. She will stiffen the neck, pull the head back and down into the shoulders, shorten and narrow the back, pull the knees together, and hold the breath until settled in a "comfortable" slump in the chair.

Now, the best way to carry out any act is to do so with a neck that is free from tension, a head that is moving forward and up away from the body, a back that is lengthening and widening, and with a free flowing of the breath. All this will ensure that the integrity of the head-neck-back relationship is maintained. The act is then done with minimum muscular effort. There is also another particular benefit: an adequate supply of blood to the brain.

How does one go about changing habitual, harmful ways of moving and being? The answer is that we should learn how to *think* or *direct* the body into new, co-ordinated, beneficial experiences that involve conscious awareness of the co-ordinated "means," the "how" of doing something, no matter how trivial or irksome. The small tasks of our everyday lives deserve as much attention as the great ones. For so much of the day we do these very things—sitting, standing, walking, resting, breathing, or sleeping—and fail to remember the importance of doing them in a co-ordinated way. These functions are usually done in the wrong way for a whole lifetime.

Where do I begin, you ask? To repeat: We should first learn how to *inhibit* or *stop* our old harmful habits, or we can't learn new and better ones. This process of inhibition is absolutely fundamental to the process of real change. Without it, any attempts at change will be like merely moving furniture around and not striking at the root of the problem.

Let us take a basic example to help clarify these statements. A person is being taught constructive awareness by a competent teacher. The teacher begins by asking the person to sit down but, before doing so, to stop and consider the best means of gaining the end of being seated in the chair.

As stated earlier, the poise of the head, the freedom of the neck, the posture of the spine, and the function of the breath determine every attitude of the whole body. In anything we do, the integrity of the head-neck-back relationship should be maintained. It is the central, unifying reflex mechanism in the body. The quality of this relationship determines the quality of our being and doing, the quality of our living.

The poise of the head is determined by the state of the neck muscles. If they are tensed and shortened, the head will be pulled back and down into the shoulders as a cultivated habit. So, to improve the quality of the movement of sitting down, one has to simply inhibit or stop the tension in the neck muscles. This simple act of inhibiting, however, is the great difficulty to be overcome in the process of change. Most people find that it is impossible, without the help of the teacher, to resist the habit of stiffening the neck muscles and displacing the head.

Why is this so? The reason is that the desire to gain the end of sitting in the chair is so strong that one cannot keep one's attention on the "means," which involve allowing the neck to stay free and the head to go forward and up. "End-gaining" is a universal modern habit. Life is so fast and stressful that we spend our days striving endlessly to get things done quickly. Misusing our psycho-physical mechanisms in the process, we remain unaware of the damage we do to ourselves spiritually, mentally, emotionally, and physically—usually until it is too late.

We can now return to the start of the journey from standing to sitting and use the co-ordinated "means" of achieving our end. The person decides to sit down and, in order to be constructively aware of this co-ordinated "means" of doing so, instantly inhibits any movement until she *thinks* or *directs* her neck to be free and her head to go forward and up. She makes no movement at all until this thought/direction is clearly formed in her mind. Having made it so, she can then allow the knees to move forward and the hips to move back, while maintaining, *as the first priority*, the conscious directions to the neck and head, all the way through the movement from standing to sitting.

On paper this process seems simple. But if you try it by yourself, you will find it impossible to perform without reverting to your old habit of stiffening your neck and pulling your head back and down into your shoulders. For the vast majority of people, this conscious process of inhibition and direction is simply impossible without the help of a competent teacher to guide them.

The process of being in the moment, keeping this constructive awareness, is an indispensable part of any attempt to live a more spiritual life. Not only must our knowledge of the working of the external world be linked to the knowledge of the working of the psycho-physical organism, it must also be linked to what we actually know about the working of the spiritual world. To what avail are our attempts to prematurely pierce the veil of the beyond or discover what happens after death, when we have not solved the problem of our so-called mundane existence in the present moment? The unity of the mind-body relationship should be raised to a more elevated position if we are to progress spiritually and in the practical affairs of everyday living.

The illustration of conscious sitting is but one example of physical movement that can be applied to the whole gamut of human activity. It would, however, be a mistake to assume that the process has primarily to do with bodywork. It does not. It concerns chiefly how to *think* about not only *what* you are doing, but *how* you are doing it. It concerns how to "think in activity" whether that activity be mental, physical, emotional, or a combination of all three. It is first and foremost a *mental* process, which involves taking that step into the unknown mentioned earlier.

Even the supposedly simple act of sitting down in an unfamiliar but co-ordinated way (as the pupil has been carefully guided into by the teacher with consent) causes fear and anxiety in many people—often to the extent that they cannot move at all—because the new situation feels entirely wrong. The pupil's intellectual grasp of what is to be done in order to execute the new, co-ordinated movement is of no avail. Only when the pupil is guided gently by the teacher, only when the act is repeated often enough, does the pupil's fear begin to subside and the intellectual "knowledge" of the new movement become *real* knowledge gained through *experience*.

This process of inhibition isn't something hanging in the air of a doubtful, vague, metaphysical flight of fancy. It is a physical fact of the nervous system, a fact that has been established by medical science.

I shall give but a brief outline of the role of inhibition in the nervous system, as a comprehensive one is not necessary for the purpose of this book. Messages travel along the nerves by means of an electro-chemical process. Within the brain and from the brain to other parts of the nervous system exists a vast, complex system of neurons, some of which are excited into action and others which inhibit action. This system gives us the ability to make a movement or to not make a movement. Inhibition of messages is just as important—nay, even more important if we wish to effect real change—than the passing-on of messages.

The problem for us as modern people is that our lives are so geared to "end-gaining" that our excitatory neurons are being stimulated all the time into habitual activity. The brain reacts to our thoughts in the same way, sending the same messages along the same nerve pathways, causing our muscles to react in a way that outwardly can be recognized as habitual behavior. This is the neurophysiological fact of a habit, which can be described as the manifestation of a constant.

Our power to inhibit, as a result, has fallen into disuse. We now should learn how to bring this inhibition from the subconscious to the conscious level. This is the *indirect* process mentioned briefly in chapter two, which is the basis of real change, the gateway to real change.

By 1949, medical science had established and accepted inhibition as a vital function of the nervous system, although one prominent Australian neurophysiologist was still vehemently denying its existence. It was, however, discovered in the most practical way through human *experience* as far back as the last decade of the nineteenth century, and has been used ever since by a growing number of people interested in making radical, conscious, constructive change in themselves.

I use the word "radical" to emphasize that in order to change, we should first learn how to *inhibit*; we should *know* how to *stop* at the source, all our old, harmful habits of misusing our psychophysical organism. With many modern systems that profess to bring about real change in the individual, a person can learn how to change from a brown cow to a white cow, but still remains a cow. Through inhibition one can change from a cow to a horse.

There are two main reasons why humanity has progressed to the evolutionary stage we are now at. One is the tremendous *need* to do, to know, to develop and to change; the other is our ability to be *creative* in this process. The conscious mind possesses limitless inquisitiveness and creativity. It is the great driving force behind our need to do, to know, to develop, to change, and to create. Through this need, the so-called subconscious mind has created all the various organs of the body required for our development. This shows that creativity is not confined to artists, musicians, authors, etc., but is a vital fact of the constitution of every human being. Some people are more creative than others simply because they have developed certain talents through many lifetimes. Why can a child prodigy do such wonderful things at a very early age? She is merely picking up from the point at which she left off in her last life.

The relationship of the conscious to the subconscious mind at our present stage of human progress is worth considering here. One of the main aims in Yoga, for example, is to become master of one's body. Many tales exist about amazing powers developed by Yogis—powers such as the ability to stop the heartbeat or to drink poison with no ill effects. Such practices, however, are highly dangerous when the conscious mind interferes with a subconscious function that has been perfected over millions of years and which continues at its best when left alone.

There is a recorded case of a Yogi who could drink poison with no ill effects, because his specific control of the digestive system was so good that he could hold the poison in check in his stomach and it was not released into his bloodstream. After holding the poison for a few minutes of the utmost concentration, he would discretely regurgitate it. Tragically, however, he died while demonstrating this feat to an audience which became so excited that he could not get clear of the people and was unable to prevent the poison from entering his bloodstream.

A developed Yogi's ability to control parts of his or her body is certainly to be wondered at. But such skills involve specific controls which can only be maintained for a short time. The natural, subconscious processes of digestion or heartbeat will reassert themselves, as they are more powerful than the conscious mind's ability to alter or affect them. This type of specific control not only can be a dangerous form of trickery; it also indicates a misunderstanding of the relationship between the conscious and the subconscious parts of the mind. If we wish to become masters of our own bodies, a more reasonable approach is needed, as well as a better understanding of this conscious-subconscious relationship.

If we consider the state of the conscious mind in the modern day, we find that in the last three hundred years or so it has expanded more than it did in the preceding two million years. Our technological advancement due to the rapid growth of the conscious mind is truly amazing, but this brought us many problems. Prominent among these problems is our frantic habit of "end-gaining," which interferes with our ability to attend to the co-ordinated "means" of carrying out our daily activities.

"What is the path?" the Zen master Nan-sen was asked.
"Everyday life is the path," he answered.

The sorry state of the world shows with tragic clarity that the vast majority of the human race cannot cope with the ever-accelerating changes which are now going on. We are in a state of constantly increasing anxiety due to this unbalanced advancement of the conscious mind, which causes tremendous muscle tension in the body and forces it to become distorted and misused. Misuse leads to malfunction which leads to illness. In short, the body cannot cope with the rapid changes in modern civilization, due to the "end-gaining" habit of the ever-expanding conscious mind.

Let us explore another example of the relationship of the conscious to the subconscious part of the mind. Many theories exist as to how we have developed through millions of years of evolution. Did we branch off from the apes? Did we come out of the sea? etc. No matter our origin, it is reasonable to suggest that our power of smell has reached its present sophisticated level in the following manner.

At one time back in the evolutionary darkness, the creature went around sniffing absolutely everything to ensure that no danger existed to life and limb. This process was carried out with relentless repetition until, at some point, some bright individual decided it was not necessary to check everything because not all things were dangerous to its welfare. The creature then felt a need to develop something in the body to monitor odors in a way that would free the conscious mind of the tyranny of having to pay attention to every single smell, thus allowing it to attend to other things. This recognition of a need caused the creative process of developing the olfactory lobes, which would monitor smells at the subconscious level; this process was repeated over and over, until the olfactory lobes were perfected.

This subconscious process continues in us today. As you read these lines, your olfactory lobes are monitoring each smell that comes to you; but it is not necessary for the conscious mind to pay attention to them until a danger signal registers, for example, the smell of smoke which tells you that your house is on fire!

The great immediate need for humanity is to learn how to use the psycho-physical organism in a manner that will bring balance, co-ordination, and ease of movement to the body as well as harmonious, reasoned behavior, emotional stability, and a greater degree of happiness to the mind. Too many people too often try to change the lives of others, without realizing that the first place to start is with themselves. "Love your neighbor *as yourself*" is the great maxim, but the last two words of this exhortation are usually forgotten.

As in the past, through many lifetimes, the individual can meet this need by creative thinking, which will bring positive, radical change. As stated earlier, this change can be effected through the inhibition of our old, harmful, subconscious habits and tendencies. The conscious mind can then direct the body through creative thinking into mechanically appropriate ways of posture and movement; but it can only do so if it realizes that the various natural processes that go on in the body, such as the beating of the heart and the functioning of the digestive system, must be left to the wisdom of the subconscious mind. By striking a balance between the functions of the conscious and subconscious parts of the mind, one can truly become master of one's own body.

The creative role of the conscious mind will now be examined in more detail. Within the body there exists a host of postural reflexes which, if left alone, would keep the body gracefully erect and allow it to move smoothly and easily in keeping with the Greek ideal of beauty. As mentioned earlier, however, the body of the modern human being suffers from generations of misuse caused by fear and anxiety, which bring all kinds of problems, prominent among them being the interference with the balance of these postural reflexes.

The term "reflex" must be emphasized here. If we are to allow the body to perform at its co-ordinated best, we should stop interfering with these reflexes and release them into activity, the activity which they know best how to perform. This means that through using constructive awareness we learn that there is nothing to do *directly* to bring about positive change. For the body to stand easily erect is not a "doing," but a function of the postural reflexes which the conscious mind must *allow* by getting itself out of the way. This it does by thinking the head-neck-back relationship into a more balanced situation which (because this relationship is the primary, unifying, reflex mechanism in the body) will improve, in process, the other support reflexes. Thus again, we see that there is nothing for the individual to *do*, in order to change, but plenty to think and allow.

Let us return to the person who stoops habitually in standing and attempts to change this by directly pulling herself up to a more erect situation. We can now understand that she cannot maintain this new height for long because in achieving it she has used the same habitual "doing" that she brings to the performance of every other act. No fundamental change can be effected in this way, because the postural reflexes have not been released to perform their proper function of keeping the body erect with the minimum of effort.

Her ineffective direct method should be replaced by the

indirect process of inhibiting the old, habitual "doing" and then consciously thinking or directing the body to lengthen up into an erect situation by releasing the postural reflexes. This will bring about the optimal, balanced relationship of the head to the neck and the neck to the torso.

The power of *thinking* must be emphasized again. Everything we do in our daily activities is done because we think it first and then do it. Take walking as an example: If we wish to walk down the street, we have to think "walking"; otherwise we will be doing something else, like sitting, or standing or whatever. The conscious mind thinks "walk" first, and then the subconscious mind responds by activating the neurons, nerves, and muscles needed to meet the *wish* of the conscious mind. Walking easily is something we have learned over millions of years—again through dreadful repetition, in a fashion similar to that of smelling—so that the act of walking does not have to be at the forefront of our attention as we do it. While walking, we can talk to a friend at the same time, but nevertheless we are thinking "walking" even as we talk.

Not only the power but the supreme place of thinking must be here underlined. In my teaching experience, it is obvious that many people do not appreciate its power. Here is an example that I encounter often in my work. I ask a person to make a specific movement only after first inhibiting the habitual impulse. I explain that when I ask her to "sit down," for example, she is first to refuse to respond to my words (stimulus). After she has thus inhibited her immediate habitual response, she is to form a clear direction to her body into the new co-ordinated "means" of executing the movement. It is obvious from her reaction to this suggestion that she doubts the effectiveness of her thinking in the situation. She has either forgotten, or has never been aware of the miracle she performs day after day in her life of doing things because she thinks about them first.

It is a sad fact of human existence that this miracle is taken for granted. We remain divided beings because we are habitually unable to bridge the gap between the intangible, ethereal thinking of the mind and the apparently physical body. The glamour of the "materiality" of the body and the world in which it moves are truly mesmerizing.

We forget that mind is our essence. We forget, or do not know, that a so-called *mere* thought does initiate so-called physical movement, does excite millions of neurons into activity in the nervous system, which brings about electrochemical reactions of amazing complexity, resulting in the execution of the act we *wish* to perform. In view of this, it should not be so difficult for us to appreciate that the power of thinking will affect the inhibitory neurons, exciting activity in them, which will stop our old sub-conscious tendencies and penetrate to the very heart of habitual, harmful behavior. This is truly the gateway to change.

This chapter can be summed up by saying that inhibiting our old, harmful habits of our use of the psycho-physical-emotional-spiritual organism is the basis of real change, the gateway to change. We can then learn to think or direct the body and mind into a state of balance and co-ordination, both in posture and movement during the everyday activities of life. This procedure can truly teach us how to be in the moment, how to be construc-tively aware of the best "means" of doing anything, no matter how trivial. It still allows us to consider things like the after-death state, for example, and deeper questions like "What am I?" without losing one iota of our practicality, that practicality which is essen-tial to a balanced existence in the here and now.

It is in the joining of mind-stilling and mind-sharpening methods that the right qualities for the discovery of truth become unfolded. Each is incomplete without the other, and therefore can lead only to partial truth.

Paul Brunton

5

MEDITATION

IMAGINE that you are attending your first class in meditation and the teacher says to the group: "Sit quietly on your cushion, cross your legs in front of you, keep your back straight, and try to still your thoughts."

To ally constructive awareness with Yoga, this chapter will begin by considering the phrase: "Keep your back straight." Most people react to this request by drawing themselves upwards as high as possible in the manner described in the previous chapter—that is, by "doing" something to render the back as straight as possible. As we have already seen, this can't be done for long because habitual misuse of the body has led to the postural reflexes not functioning properly. The person cannot escape gradually reverting to the habitual, slumped manner of sitting. The old habit is simply too strong. No amount of direct "doing" will achieve a straight back or, more correctly, a balanced, easy posture.

When we are meditating, a balanced, easy posture is highly desirable. We need the body to be as comfortable as possible so that it does not disturb the mind. Most people, however, do not possess a back strong enough to support the torso easily. They need a process of re-education in constructive awareness to achieve the state implied in that deceptively simple phrase: "Keep your back straight." Even people of the body-building school, men and women, would be shocked to discover that their backs are nowhere near as strong as they imagine. The strength achieved in the back through constructive awareness is not macho strength developed through brute force. It is a quiet endurance which is gradually built up as the postural reflexes are released and allowed to perform their proper, co-ordinated function.

The function of the postural reflexes within the field of gravity is worth noting here. It is a general misconception that gravity is the heavy burden we have to carry, the enemy that we fight unsuccessfully for a whole lifetime until it eventually lowers us into the grave. This is not so.

There exists within the body a mechanism which allows it to function in an upright situation within the gravitational field. If gravity is removed, as in the case of astronauts in space, then, contrary to expectations, the body does not lengthen and expand, it shortens and narrows. Only when gravity is restored does the space-traveler return to an erect posture. Gravity actually allows the body to expand in all directions; it is only our misconception of the use of the psycho-physical organism that causes the shortened, narrowed bodies which we see all around us.

Another common misconception is that, due to the influence of gravity and other pressures and heartaches of a lifetime, it is inevitable that we become stooped and bent in old age. This is unnecessary. A proper understanding of the use of the psycho-physical mechanism would prevent such a sad state of affairs. To avoid this exaggerated degeneration in old age would be sufficient reason for adopting constructive awareness; but it goes much deeper than this and is indispensable if we are to successfully progress mentally, physically, emotionally, and spiritually. Our progress should be an all-round one which will bring balance into our way of being. Instead of allowing ourselves to indulge in the pathetic fallacy of blaming other people and events for our psycho-physical degeneration, we can take control of our own lives through constructive awareness and see our lives become increasingly interesting as we grow older.

We can now look again at another aspect of this process of

constructive awareness which can bring greater balance, co-ordination, and happiness into our lives. This was mentioned briefly in
chapter one and concerns the difference between two desirable
phases of the mind, one being that of extroverted attention and
the other introverted concentration.

The concentration of the mind in meditation is in contrast to,
but not antipathetic to, the expansion of attention in the waking
state. Both are functions of the mind. The former seeks to still the
mind during meditation, the latter to render it as active and aware
as possible during the interaction of the self with the environment
in the everyday, repetitive tasks of the waking state.

Let us consider the state of extroverted attention first. This is
the ideal state in which to deal with the world in our everyday
activities, because it concerns the *form* side of life, not its *essence*.
This state, however, is actually not commonly enjoyed by the
modern person. Most people attempt to "concentrate," that is, to
concentrate on one thing to the exclusion of everything else—
including what is actually happening to the body during the
period of concentration. This way of concentrating is generally
considered to be highly desirable in order to pay adequate
attention to important things like study, work, sport, playing a
musical instrument, and so on. Numerous well-worn phrases
abound: "You must learn to concentrate." "Keep your mind on the
job." "You must bring the mind to bear on the subject." "Don't let
your mind wander."

In the meantime, the poor body is usually in a fixed, slumped
situation with a stiffened neck, a head falling backward (or forward) and down, a back that is shortening and narrowing, legs
that are crossed, a pair of lungs that cannot breathe properly because of the restricted condition of the rib cage, as well as vital
organs which are being squashed and are, therefore, unable to
function adequately. None of this is conducive to true concen-
trated thinking. It will certainly not allow any inspired thinking,
geniuses excepted, because the body has an influence on the
mind; if the body is functioning below its best, it will adversely

weaken the power of the mind to think. This type of concentration is, in fact, a kind of self-hypnosis which severely limits the mind because we attempt to exclude everything else, including the body, from our field of awareness. The fact that the human being is a psycho-physical unity simply does not allow such a one-sided condition. The state of extroverted attention is much more desirable and works as follows.

To achieve a balanced state conducive to deep, sustained thinking, we should bring the body into our field of awareness and set up favorable conditions in it, which will allow the mind as much freedom as possible to think and ponder. These favorable conditions begin with restoring the integrity of the head-neck-back relationship. If this primary unifying reflex mechanism in the body is functioning optimally, it will allow the other support reflexes and vital organs to do the same. This means that, even as you are thinking of a subject, you give the head-neck-back relationship priority and think about it before paying attention to the subject. Indeed, you maintain it as a priority all the way through the period of thinking. This is extroverted attention.

Let us consider a practical example. You wish to read a book while standing, and in order to use extroverted attention will follow this procedure. Before picking up the book, stop and think of not stiffening your neck, think your head forward and up, and your back to lengthen and widen. Then, while still maintaining these thoughts as an ever-present priority, pick up the book to a height where you do not need to drop your head forward to read it. Now ask yourself: Am I using the appropriate amount of muscle effort to hold the book up? Am I treating it as if it is ten times heavier than it really is? Am I tightening my shoulders? Am I pushing my hips forward? Am I bracing my knees back and tensing my legs, or just as harmfully standing on one leg and throwing the whole body out of balance? Is my breath coming easily? Having rectified all these negative conditions, you can now start reading and giving the subject matter your attention, without dropping your constructive awareness of the body. This, again, is extroverted attention. It begins with attention to the head-neck-back relationship as the highest priority. Only then is the subject matter of the book given its due consideration.

At this point, you may object that to pay attention at the same time to all the details mentioned above would be impossible. Indeed few, if any, individuals can learn this process of constructive awareness without the help of a competent teacher. The guiding thoughts or directions—for example, "the head to go forward and up" —are particularly difficult to understand and can only be fully explained by the teacher through practical demonstration in the one-to-one situation of a lesson. The process can, however, be learned with time, just as one needs time to learn how to play a musical instrument, or tennis, or whatever.

One advantage of using extroverted attention is that it increases a person's ability to stop "mind-wandering," which is one of the most destructive habits of the modern human being. The body has an influence on the mind and vice versa. It is, therefore, difficult to say whether "mind-wandering" causes misuse of the body, or conversely, misuse of the body causes "mind-wandering." But the fact remains that both of these negative habits exist in modern people, and they are instrumental in preventing us from giving adequate, sustained attention to whatever we are doing or thinking.

Television, in addition, has a tremendous, negative influence on our ability to bring our minds to bear on a subject, because most of it is geared to making it easy for us to watch and not to think too much. MTV is particularly detrimental to young people, because of the huge number of images thrown at the mind during the three minutes of a typical modern song on video. These quick-fire images tend to scatter the mind and adversely affect one's ability to pay due attention to more important subjects.

Let us now consider the other state, that of introverted concentration, a highly favorable state to achieve during meditation. Indeed, meditation is the only activity where concentration is actually welcomed, because one is attempting to slow down or even stop the incessant activity of the intellect. In this way, one attempts to exclude the external world, including the body, from one's field of awareness, in order to become aware of the deeper layers of the mind. This initial exploration of the mystical depths of the human consciousness is the sense in which the term "introverted concentration" is here used.

Nevertheless, this does not mean that we can simply ignore the body. The more unbalanced, uncoordinated, and uncomfortable the body is, the more it will impinge on the mind and obstruct our efforts to withdraw attention from our external surroundings. Just as in extroverted attention, the individual needs a process of re-education in constructive awareness to allow the body to function easily in a balanced, co-ordinated manner, free from discomfort.

This means that when one sits down to meditate, the comfort of the body is taken care of through attention to the integrity of the head-neck-back relationship. The body should be sitting easily erect before the real work of introverted concentration begins. When an individual has learned constructive awareness, the body will sit easily erect, because to do so is a *reflex* activity which does itself. It is a function of the so-called subconscious mind. The result will be, of course, that the body will not force itself on your attention as you try to still the mind. This makes the path of the spiritual seeker much smoother.

Consciousness of the Spirit is not obtained
by contortion of the legs. . . . It is better for
instance, to eat brown bread than to be able
to contort the body in yoga posture number 57!

Paul Brunton

6

HATHA YOGA

PROBABLY the most popular part of Eastern practices recently adopted by the Western world is that of Hatha Yoga or physical yoga. Many Westerners enjoy it because it is tangible and practical, unlike the more subtle and delicate pursuit of mystical meditation. One can see the physical results of efforts in Hatha Yoga as one becomes more supple and develops more control of the body. By contrast, it is not easy to measure one's progress in the deeper regions of the mind during meditation.

Let us consider some aspects of Hatha Yoga in relation to constructive awareness. One of the aims in Hatha Yoga, as practiced in the West, is to render the body as supple and lithe as possible; various curious *asanas* (postures) are adopted in order to lengthen muscles, tendons, and ligaments. Through this procedure, a certain control of the body is gained. Too many Western books on the subject, however, overemphasize the benefits from its practice and say too little about the dangers.

Two of these dangers will be considered here. The first is the most important, associated with the *asanas* that involve bending the lumbar spine to an extreme degree. Back-stretching poses such as *Paschimotasana* (sitting back-stretching pose) and *Padahastasana* (standing back-stretching pose) are two obvious examples of bending the lumbar spine forwards. *Bhujangasana* (the Cobra) and *Chakrasana* (the Wheel) are examples of bending it backwards. As stated earlier, the back is not designed primarily for bending, the hip joints are. If it is your habit to misuse the body by constantly bending the back during the thousand and one tasks of everyday life, and then you practice these *asanas* on top of that, you are in great danger of causing damage to your spine. One danger is a prolapse, or as it is more commonly known, a slipped disc.

Another example of the second danger is the Half Lotus, and even more so, the Full Lotus, where the legs are tied together in front of the sitting, erect torso. Many people attempt to meditate for a long time in these difficult positions. This is not advisable, however, as the blood supply is cut off to the legs, causing great pressure on the veins, which will be damaged and become varicose.

Speaking generally, the problem for Westerners in practicing Hatha Yoga is the old bugbear habit of "end-gaining." One looks enviously at the apparently supple, healthy Yogi performing easily the *asanas* shown in pictures and wishes fervently to emulate her. The *asanas* are then enthusiastically attempted and the body is pushed and pulled around with too much effort to gain this end of looking like the Yogi. If practicing alone, not enough consideration is given to the suitability of certain *asanas* for one's own body; if one is attending a class, consideration is not given to how much the teacher really knows about the physical benefits each *asana* is supposed to bring about.

There is another serious result to consider if one is performing *asanas* in the "end-gaining" manner by using too much force. This result is plastic deformation of the tendons and ligaments and occurs as follows. A tendon is a tough, fibrous material that connects muscle to bone. A ligament is similar and attaches bone to bone. When a muscle contracts, say to lift an arm, it pulls on the tendon, which pulls on the bone and the arm is raised. Ligaments prevent joints from being pulled apart.

The difference between muscles and tendons and muscles and ligaments is that muscles are actively controlled through the nervous system, while tendons and ligaments are not to the same degree. This means that muscles have the ability to protect themselves actively by contracting reflexly against any force which tends to stretch them too far. Tendons and ligaments can only do this passively. For these reasons, the following situation can occur. If one is using too much force in practicing an *asana*, the muscles will be actively contracting while the tendons and ligaments are being stretched beyond their elastic limit. This results in their becoming plastic, so that they are unable to return to the normal, appropriate tension needed to adequately support and protect the joints, which will become too loose. I have also taught constructive awareness to many dancers, particularly modern dancers, and have witnessed this phenomenon in them due to the extremes to which the body is forced. Injury is one of the biggest open secrets in the dance world.

The point being made here is that one may practice the *asanas* and apparently become more supple and flexible, but do so by adversely affecting the tendons and ligaments while little or no change is made to the muscles, which remain in their habitual, shortened state.

More importantly, however, this means that one has not changed one's habitual misuse of the body and remains the slave of this habitual behavior. You may now be a white cow instead of a brown one, but you're still a cow! The reason is that we cannot change our use of ourselves in this direct manner by performing Yoga *asanas* for a few hours per week or even per day. The important question of the misuse of the self during the dreadful repetition of our daily activities is not being tackled. Incidentally, the same situation is true if one performs typical strenuous Western physical exercises in the gym; one takes the same habitual misuse into the doing of them that one has in habitual, daily activity.

How should Westerners practice Hatha Yoga? Great caution should be exercised, not only in choosing which *asanas* to perform, but also in the way, or "how," of doing them. This caution applies especially to care of the lumbar spine, because damage to it can make one's life an utter misery, can bring a chronic condition of "No life, no death!"

The *asanas* should be performed easily with no "end-gaining" efforts to stretch too far, and certainly with not even a hint of pain. The Western adage applied to physical exercises "If it hurts, it's good for you," is not only wrong, it is a foolish statement. Western exercises are designed to create bulging muscles and an over-expanded chest. For the healthful development of a balanced human being, it is enough to bring the muscles no farther than the point of easy and instant obedience, to make the body perform its varied functions adequately and gracefully. Any *asana* which involves bending the back too much should be carefully considered and avoided if you think there is any danger of injury. No pose or posture should be held for too long, neither should the breath. One should avoid getting carried away with vigorous enthusiasm which results in "end-gaining."

Constructive awareness should be practiced in any and every *asana*. This entails looking at each one and asking yourself, "Does this pose contradict the proper functioning of the body as a mechanism?" If it does, then you should not practice it. As stated earlier, it is much more important to practice constructive awareness, where one uses the body in a mechanically appropriate way in the everyday acts of life.

To repeat and to emphasize, the practice of constructive awareness will give one a strong, stable, but not rigid back, with an adequate degree of flexibility. Any movements made by the body will be done by using the freedom cultivated in the big joints, namely, hips, knees, ankles, shoulders, wrists, and, most importantly, the head-neck joint. This means that the back will never be bent further than the limit that the intervertebral discs can safely manage.

A person may feel the need to practice Hatha Yoga, either for philosophical reasons or simply for enjoyment; but one should appreciate that it is not a tradition in the West. Traditional Eastern Yoga is not suited to Western people who take up the practice in later life, and an easier, modified version of it is much more desirable. Many of the traditional *asanas* are simply too difficult and hold many potential dangers. Taking up the practice in later life does not mean middle and old age only. It applies also to people in their twenties, even teens, who have developed harmful, habitual misuse of themselves.

If the hatha yogis are right, if the way to the
kingdom of heaven is nasal and atmospheric,
then why should we trouble to become unselfish,
disciplined, and intelligent? Why bother to
improve our characters at all? No! the wise
student does not need breathing exercises
although he may use them.

Paul Brunton

7

TO BREATHE, OR NOT TO BREATHE ?

THE PROFOUNDLY intimate connection between the state of one's mind and emotions, and the quality of one's breathing is easily seen. If your mind is excited, your emotions agitated, then your breathing will come in quick gasps; if you are mentally and emotionally calm, then the breath will flow quietly, evenly, and slowly. When you are suddenly startled, a quick gasp emanates from the throat; or if you are suddenly taken by the beauty of a flower or a natural scene of great grandeur, then you will say, "It took my breath away!" The breath is truly the sister of the mind.

The breathing process is a reflex activity normally controlled by the subconscious part of the mind. The conscious mind can exert a limited control over the breath, and this control can be used to advantage in meditation.

The typical mind is likened to an agitated monkey, jumping around too much and never at peace. Because of the close connection of the breath to the mind, consciously slowing the breath can calm the mind. Many books on Yoga give breathing exercises that can be used to achieve this retarded rhythm. Such exercises should be viewed with caution. Some of them are dangerous, because of the ridiculous extremes that they go to. Injury can result from them. Some Yogis, for example, have burst blood vessels in the lungs through holding the breath too long. Before considering methods of breathing, let us look firstly at the conscious and subconscious aspects of it.

As stated, breathing is, first and foremost, a reflex activity. Please take careful note of this before practicing any kind of breathing exercises. The power of this reflex activity is easily demonstrated. Give attention to your breathing for a few minutes and observe its ebb and flow. At some point, breathe out a little more than usual and then try to not allow another breath to come in for ten minutes! Or try the reverse of not allowing the breath to go out for ten minutes. You can quickly see that the conscious mind has only limited control. Attempts should not be made to exceed these limits.

The breath is not only intimately connected with the mind and the emotions, but obviously also with the body. Indeed, breath is humankind's most vital and valuable energy and should be allowed its proper function. It cannot be excluded from any scheme of change or transformation. Breathing is the medium between the mind and the body. The quality and effectiveness of its functioning depends upon our psycho-physical state which, in turn, depends upon our use of the self. One result of poor use is the shortening in length of the back, which causes the rib-cage to sag and become narrower, thus severely restricting the flow of breath (not to mention constricting the heart). In this slumped situation, the intercostal muscles are unable to fulfil their natural function of caressing and releasing the lungs.

As with other bodily functions, the quality of our breathing is determined by the head-neck-back relationship. If this relationship is not at its optimal, then we cannot breathe adequately. No matter whether we practice gentle or violent breathing exercises, their effectiveness will always remain limited if we do not restore the integrity of the head-neck-back relationship. This proviso applies also to any breathing exercises which purport to restore health. They can yield only limited benefits because they deal with a specific aspect of one's being and functioning and not with the being as a whole.

In the process of constructive awareness, we do not advocate breathing exercises as a chief undertaking; but we do advocate setting up proper, balanced, physical conditions in the body which will allow the reflex action of the breathing mechanism to function at its best. These conditions are brought about by *thinking* or *directing* the primary unifying reflex mechanism—that is, the head-neck-back relationship—into its optimal, dynamic situation. The natural, reflex action of the breathing will then be the indirect result of the improvement in the primary head-neck-back relationship.

How does this happen? A fully-detailed physiological explanation is not possible here, but let us review a few basic facts.

The intervertebral discs exert hydraulic pressure on the vertebrae above and below them, the power of this pressure being determined by the amount of fluid at the center of the discs. One of the functions of the body during sleep is the absorption of more fluid into the discs, so that one is taller on rising in the morning than on going to bed the previous night. This means also that the back muscles will have lengthened in response. When the upthrust in the discs is balanced by appropriate tension or pull in the muscles, a strong, dynamic back is produced. This improved situation is effected through the conscious process of constructive awareness.

The head sits on top of the spine and is connected to it, as well as to other parts of the body, by muscles. All muscles function by pulling, they cannot push. When the spine lengthens, the head will be pushed upwards in space. Through its string-like, muscular connections to the shoulder-girdle and rib-cage, the head will pull these parts upward with it, thus relieving the unnecessary pressure on the heart, lungs, and other vital organs in the torso. In other words, when the spine is restored to its optimal length, the shoulder-girdle and the rib-cage will be suspended from the head; this co-ordinated situation will allow the spontaneous, reflex functioning of the breathing mechanism. This will obviously contribute positively to our general health and well-being, due to the fact that health and strength are, to a certain extent, in ratio to lung power.

Many misconceptions exist about the functioning of the breathing, prominent among them being so-called "low-breathing" into the abdominal area. The process of breathing is done mainly through the co-ordinated reflex action of the intercostal muscles and the diaphragm, not by the abdominal muscles. In balanced breathing, the abdomen moves appropriately in and out in response to the up and down movements of the diaphragm. It is physiologically and anatomically impossible to breathe into the abdomen. The abdominal muscles, like the neck muscles, are utilized by the subconscious mind for breathing only in an emergency situation where the intercostal muscles and the diaphragm cannot function properly.

Incidentally, "low-breathing" into the abdomen is taught and used very much in "serious" singing, where many students are instructed to think of the support for the torso coming from this area. Adequate abdominal pressure, however, can come only when the spine is at its full length and the torso, as a whole, is lengthening and widening. The support from the abdomen is a popular misconception in the world of song. I have witnessed and worked with many singers who have cultivated the harmful situation where the rib-cage is expanded in an attempt to breathe optimally, but gets fixed, by undue muscle tension, in this position, forcing the diaphragm to move up and down excessively to compensate. This unbalanced, rigid situation prevents the intercostal muscles from performing their natural function of alternately caressing and releasing the lungs to allow them to inhale and exhale.

Let us return to our consideration of the connection between the mind and the breath, particularly in relation to meditation. That agitated monkey, the modern intellect, is most difficult to control, discipline, and quieten. When one sits down to meditate, the ego starts running frantically around and comes up with thoughts about the most trivial or most fantastic things. It does this to prevent itself from facing what lies behind and beyond it. Slowing the breath helps to slow the intellect and stop the ego from indulging in this frantic activity.

How should a person slow down the rhythm of the breath-cycle? Start by sitting quietly and allow the breathing to function easily through the nose. If the back is not strong enough to support itself comfortably, then allow it to be supported by the back of an upright chair.

Observe the in-and-out flow of the breath. To deepen as well as slow the breath, the following procedure can be adopted. At some point, as the breath is flowing outward, consciously but gently prolong it for a few seconds. The in-breath should then be *allowed* to happen and will naturally be a little longer and deeper than normal, as a reaction to the prolongation of the out-breath. It is totally unnecessary to "take a breath," as is done habitually in most breathing exercises. If you "take a breath," then the breathing is turned into a "doing" by the conscious mind, instead of an "allowing" by the reflex action of the subconscious mind. The out-breath, of course, is also a reflex action; but to alter the rhythm of the breath, it is best to start with the conscious prolongation of the out-breath.

We should also consider how we breathe during our everyday activities—going about those menial tasks in that relatively quiet, easy manner which does not make a big demand on the breathing process. In these situations, it is advisable to cultivate nostril breathing, that is, allowing the breath to move in and out through the nose. Too many of us breathe habitually through the mouth, which means that the air is not warmed, dried, and filtered before entering the lungs.

Nostril breathing can also be cultivated in ordinary speech. If you observe someone who is about to speak to you, you will notice that before she begins she will suck a breath in through the mouth. This is an almost universal habit which is unnecessary. The amount of breath needed for ordinary speech can be supplied easily by the breathing mechanism. Such an intake of breath occurs sharply at each pause which she has to make before carrying on with her discourse, and is usually a sign of nervousness or an exaggerated, "end-gaining" desire to say it all too quickly.

When a person is talking excitedly, this habitual sucking-in of the breath can be done to such an extent that she "loses her breath" and has to pause a while longer in order to gather it. This habit of mouth breathing can be seen even in the person who speaks calmly and quietly. It is better to speak in an easy way which will allow you to pause quietly for a moment during speech, and allow the breath to come in reflexly through the nose. This procedure makes for clearer speech, as well as giving the listener time to digest what is being said.

The "suspension system" referred to earlier will allow a more co-ordinated use of the vocal mechanism, both in ordinary speech and singing. The vocal mechanism will also be suspended from the head via the muscles connecting from it to the hyoid bone; but this can only occur when the spine is at its full length, the person having gone through the re-educative process of constructive awareness.

Referring again to breathing exercises, this chapter ends with a warning that any breathing exercise which the reader may wish to practice for any particular purpose should never be forced, strong, or violent. The breath can be deep and long, but gentle; so gentle that, if a feather were held up in front of the nose, it would not be disturbed.

Many breathing techniques exist which profess to aid progress in meditation or health. Mental and physical dangers attend the practice of wrong exercises or the wrong practice of many others. I am not offering any kind of breathing exercise whatsoever: It is entirely the choice of each individual as to which exercise he or she wishes to adopt. My concern here is to explain the vital connection between the specific process of breathing and the *general* use, good or bad, of the psycho-physical organism.

Man's success in using his knowledge of the
working of the external world can come only if
it is linked with the knowledge of the working
of his own psycho-physical mechanism and
function. For if the first leads him into self-
destruction, as it is now doing, the second
can control and safeguard him against such
an ill destiny.

Paul Brunton

8

SENSORY APPRECIATION

THERE is a problem, perhaps the greatest of all, certainly the most immediate, which humankind has to solve if permanent benefits for all—be they mental, physical, material, emotional, or spiritual—are to be realized. This problem is that of our faulty sensory appreciation, the most serious symptom of our inability to adjust to the accelerating demands of modern civilization.

Psycho-physical activity, our daily "doing," is our response to stimuli received through the senses of sight, hearing, touch, taste, and smell. The quality of perceptions and conceptions formed through this process, as well as the nature of reaction to these stimuli, is determined by the standard of psycho-physical functioning of each individual, at any given time. In other words, our abilities to apprehend with the mind, perception, and to form an idea in the mind, conception, are dependent upon the quality of our general psycho-physical use and functioning. The dependence of these processes on our general psycho-physical condition is of paramount importance, because all perceptions and conceptions are influenced by sensory processes. In every case, the nature of our reaction—whether it be an actual physical movement, an emotion, an opinion, or a belief—will be determined by the concerted activity, in action and reaction, of the processes of perception, conception, and other mechanisms which produce the "feeling" or "thought-emotion" that we experience. This concerted activity can be termed *sensory appreciation*.

Another equally important sense which constitutes one of

these other mechanisms and also functions concurrently with those already mentioned, is proprioception. This process applies to sensory nerves which serve muscles, tendons, joints, and the middle ear. Information travels back and forth from these places to the brain and tells us, not only about the interaction between one part of the body and another, but also of the body's interaction with the environment. This process is really our sixth sense. The universal incidence of misuse of the psycho-physical mechanism in the modern world indicates all too clearly how badly this sense is ignored, neglected, and misunderstood.

In an organism suffering from misuse, the general sensory appreciation (not just proprioception) is extremely faulty. Such a person's beliefs about how he or she uses the mind-body complex in everyday life are questionable, to say the least.

The relativity of subjective faculties and objective phenomena, already mentioned in chapter one, constitutes human experience in the waking state. A study of both the subjective and objective elements of relativity reveals that what we perceive has neither more nor less reality than our perception. The world of our every-day experience is not what it appears to be. It is the great illusion which is paradoxically the real.

The world is experienced through the senses, through our awareness of movement and location, through our states of con-sciousness. These elements, therefore, of the psycho-physical self constitute such essential factors in our world of experience that objects which stand outside the body cannot be separated from them. Senses and sensed objects are an indivisible unity. Again, things cannot stand alone in isolation; they must be perceived by some mind. In considering the relativity of subjectivity and objec-tivity, we cannot *assume* that so-called things which appear to be "out there" in space possess any self-identical extension at all in-dependently of the relational factors in perception.

True recognition of the inexorable relativity, both of subjective faculties and of objective phenomena, is a significant and disturb-ing event. The uneasy feeling which it brings has a genuine basis:

Deep within ourselves we sense that the faculties which we have developed, and are currently using, are untrustworthy vehicles for ultimate truth. This situation creates an urgent need in us to discover a more reliable means to knowledge.

The previous paragraph refers to the evolutionary development of our faculties and obviously means that even if they were functioning at their best, *they would still be unreliable vehicles for ultimate truth*. We must, and will, develop far finer faculties which will progressively allow us to realize ultimate truth; but at this point in time it is true that, due to defective sensory appreciation caused by the universal misuse of the psycho-physical self, the faculties presently at our disposal are functioning well beneath their potential. The first step we should take, then, is the restoration to complete reliability of these faculties. As stated earlier, we have faced neither a greater nor a more immediate problem than this. While I am not suggesting that the achievement of accurate, reliable sensory appreciation, will lead, at this time, to "ultimate truth," it will certainly provide "a more reliable means to knowledge."

Let us consider how reliable sensory appreciation can do this. We will begin by noting that the human sensory make-up is deteriorating. It is becoming more and more untrustworthy, because the effects of rapid changes in the modern civilized world are very harmful when compared to the slow, gradual ones of the past.

How did our sensory awareness go wrong in the first place? This is a very difficult question. It is reasonable to suggest that at some point in our evolutionary history some genius had the first abstract thought—perhaps a vague realization that she was more than an animal totally controlled by subconscious reactions to the various stimuli of the environment. Up to that point in time, her conscious mind had been almost exclusively involved in the building-up of her psycho-physical organism. The conscious mind became able to switch and expand its attention to a meaningful understanding of itself as an individual as well as a meaningful understanding of that self's relationship with the world. This switch, this new realization, must have been a tremendous psychological moment.

This crucial moment when the human being began to reason and analyze also signaled the start of the decline in our use of the "physical" body. At this point our attention began to be deflected from it. We ignored it more and more as our abstract thinking increased to the amazing degree that we now enjoy in the present day. This mental growth has been achieved, however, at high cost, because the excellent use that the body had enjoyed was sacrificed. The results of this can be seen throughout the modern world.

Deterioration in the co-ordination of the body brought a simultaneous decline in our sensory appreciation. The latter is now so unsatisfactory that most of us are unaware of what we actually *do* with the body in any of the multitudinous acts of our daily lives. Restoration of accurate sensory appreciation is, as already stated, the first step we have to take to obtain "a more reliable means to knowledge." This is of the utmost importance. Learning constructive awareness, co-ordinated use of the mind-body complex, will restore our sensory appreciation to greater accuracy and reliability.

Whether or not the above "history" is true does not affect the evidence before our modern eyes of the appalling, widespread decline of the physical body and the accompanying deterioration in our sensory appreciation. Today we attempt to cultivate the potentialities of "mind," "body," and "soul" but have not seen the need for maintaining satisfactory sensory appreciation, the channel through which these potentialities must express themselves.

What exactly do I mean by unsatisfactory sensory appreciation? Simply put: A particular stimulus brings a reaction that registers in one's senses quite differently than what has actually happened. Ask a person to sit down, for example. In doing so she will, among other things, stiffen and shorten the neck muscles. When this and other things are pointed out to her, she expresses surprise—even to the point of denying that she did so.

General misuse and consequent malfunctioning of our psycho-physical organism affects our ability to register sensations and experiences. We are now at a point collectively where our subconscious, habitual behavior no longer meets our needs with regard to self-improvement of any kind. Despite thousands of years of apparently wise words from the philosophers, few have come up with real, practical procedures that can be adopted and applied to daily living. Most have produced intangible theories with no practical value. Constructive awareness fills this gap. Without it, our theories and beliefs about things, both outside and inside ourselves, fail because, due to defective sensory equipment, we are unable to put our theories into practice effectively. The individual is central to all experiences, and our defective psycho-physical functioning and sensory awareness are what prevent us from bridging the gap between theory and practice.

A rational, scientific attitude toward this problem is absolutely essential. As John Dewey says "Any sound plan must prove its soundness in reference to concrete consequences and to general principles. Any theory or principle must be judged by its results in operation and must provide a method for making evident and observable what its consequences are and guarantee that these consequences flow from the principle." When judged by this standard, constructive awareness, constructive re-education, is scientific in the strictest sense.

"Life is too complex" is the excuse of the modern human being. But we should not indulge in the pathetic fallacy of blaming "life" for our ailments. We should realize instead that while we are complex creatures, good use of the organism is a simple act. Adequate development of the individual, spiritual or otherwise, requires a better standard of co-ordination of the psycho-physical mechanisms. Being content with our state, or life-condition, means that we will be unaware of our defects and will not progress. An attempt to learn something, be it the rudiments of 'rithmetic or the mysteries of mentalism, is the natural response to a wish to do so; a satisfactory result depends on satisfactory direction and control of the organism. The present-day lack of this direction and control limits our ability to learn anything because it manifests as "mind-wandering," or "not keeping our minds on the job."

Sensory appreciation is the factor we depend on for guidance in our subconscious attempts to learn something, or to use our organisms; it has an enormous influence for good or bad in our mental, physical, emotional, and spiritual development.

Another speculative glance into the early, uncivilized stage of our evolution is now necessary. The subconscious behavior which guided the human being then, together with her excellent sensory appreciation and physical condition, were sufficient to meet her needs in the almost unchanging routine of her daily life. It is almost beyond the power of the modern person to comprehend that the experiences of millions of years, over thousands of lifetimes, had gone into the building-up of this so-called physical development. The experiences we had gained on the so-called mental side were infinitesimal in comparison.

The advent of reason signaled the beginning of the end of instinct as the dominant factor in human life. But we did not realize that this instinct, which had developed so slowly over millions of years, was now inadequate for guiding us satisfactorily in the new civilized environment which was changing with increasing rapidity. The development of our "mental" powers caused a neglect of our "physical" powers, which in turn caused a speedy decline in our sensory awareness.

This situation continued until, in the later civilizing stage, the human being recognized this tremendous deterioration on the "physical" side and "physical exercises" were adopted as a remedy. The importance, however, of the interrelation and interdependence of the mechanisms of the mind-body complex was not recognized, and "mental" activity continued to increase to the detriment of balanced psycho-physical development.

The adoption of physical exercises is an example of humankind's faulty sensory appreciation and erroneous conceptions showing unbalanced judgment. They generally are based on the "end-gaining" principle of "cure," which ignores the "means" principle as a preventive measure. "Cures" for this and that are not the answer to our problems; right thinking is the world's great need. The unbalanced state which we have now reached shows little evolutionary progress from that of Stone Age Man. Indeed, in terms of violence, we have gone backwards. The incredible number of wars that have raged in the twentieth century, together with the devilish sophistication of modern weaponry, confirms all too clearly that we are capable of a hideous brutality that outstrips the "evil" of our prehistoric ancestors.

This reliance on blind, subconscious behavior is not only evident in our choice of physical exercises as a universal cure. It also characterizes our uncoordinated attempts to execute them. Due to faulty sensory appreciation, this blindness has resulted in the modern person being the most imperfectly co-ordinated creature in the history of humankind—we see our deterioration as a muscular one only, and not as a general psycho-physical one. We have overlooked the fact that all our attempts to remedy our defects have failed because their effectiveness has been measured by imperfect and delusive sensory appreciation, itself caused by the decline in our co-ordinated use of the psycho-physical self. The "remedy" idea has been geared to "gaining an end," the "means" being totally unrecognized. In adopting physical exercises, we not only failed to recognize that most of them are mechanically inappropriate, and therefore detrimental to our general well-being; we also took into the doing of them the same uncoordinated use of the organism as we employed in all our other repetitive, daily acts. Real change, real psycho-physical improvement, can come only through working to the "means" principle—which entails working against a habit of life.

We have reasoned out how to use the varied forces we have discovered in the outside world, but we have not applied this principle to ourselves. One need only walk the streets of London, New York, Berlin, or any other major city of the world to witness the truth of this statement. Misuse is rife. Specific remedies are used instead of a general, preventive principle. We have made the error of separating the organism into "body," "mind," and "soul" and yet still expect a divided being to function satisfactorily. This is unreasonable thinking.

"Mind" and "soul" are conceived as ethereal, but the body is tangible. As the the only tangible one of these three distinctions, should it not occupy the highest rather than the lowest place of importance? Why was this lowest place assigned to it by religious people, for example, even to the point of castigation?

I do not mean to imply that the deep mysteries of "mind" and "soul" should not be studied. Such study is a vital part of the life of a spiritual seeker, and life is all the richer for doing so. But any worthwhile philosophy will tell you that it is not overconcerned about things such as after-death states, or how many angels can sit on the point of a needle. It will emphasize that our first priority should be to give attention to what is happening in the present moment. Our studies on any spiritual path must include the body within such a first priority.

We must learn how to stop and cultivate, even in the tumult of late twentieth-century life, a simple, conscious way of living. Realizing the unity in all things, we should act accordingly in a practical manner. Inhibiting old, harmful habits and tendencies, while cultivating other positive new ideas and discoveries of the fertile mind of the modern human being, will allow us to do this.

We have believed in miracles and instant fixes for too long, instead of being guided by reason. This has brought tragedy in our past attempts to progress in civilization. To rise above the complex difficulties with which we are now struggling, we must establish reliable sensory appreciation in ourselves. One of the biggest reasons for the disasters which have befallen the world is the fact that our leaders have been, and still are, maladjusted, uncoordinated beings. The history of our social plan of the last three hundred years or so is replete with attempts to effect reforms based on short-term specific "end-gaining" principles which, even when achieved, have led to more complications. We seem to be completely unable to find a long view which eventually would bring real benefits for all. One way to achieve such benefits is to make constructive awareness the most fundamental, vital part of children's education. Balanced psycho-physical development is impossible without it.

Sensory Appreciation and Learning

Let us now consider sensory appreciation in relation to learning. A person's ability to learn something is based on the conception she has of what is required of her by the teacher, as expressed by the teacher's spoken or written words. The accuracy of her conception depends on the quality of psycho-physical use and functioning and of sensory appreciation present. Our first consideration, therefore, must be to secure the highest possible standard of psycho-physical functioning for the children and the teacher.

The problem today is that the debauched sensory awareness of the modern person causes harmful and abnormal reactions. Our emphasis on specific development in orthodox education means "mental" development, instead of a general development in relation to the child's organism as a whole. The situation is complicated further by the fact that children have developed many psycho-physical defects by the time they start school.

Further, teachers are usually unaware of their own poor functioning, as well as the children's poor functioning in this regard. They do not understand that the child's failure to carry out the teacher's instruction stems from relying on defective sensory awareness which has developed through misuse of the organism since very early childhood.

Children enter school at an early age and, because of the kind of suppressive discipline they experience, reach adolescence with many retarding features: uncontrolled emotions, fixed prejudices, and harmful habits. The child's fear reflexes are excited because of the system of having to pass examinations. The "end-gaining" principle prevails. No attempt is made to re-adjust and co-ordinate the children by the process of constructive awareness, which would allow them to develop to that standard of psycho-physical use which is essential to the fullest development of latent possibilities.

As mentioned earlier, the quality of an individual's perceptions and conceptions is determined her psycho-physical condition, which in turn determines the effectiveness of her sensory awareness. This means that every stimulus she receives through the senses, every idea formed in her mind, will be colored or affected by the quality of her sensory appreciation at any given time. Every reaction, opinion, belief, etc., she may have is based on sensory appreciation. Perceptions and conceptions which are influenced by unreliable sensory appreciation are incorrect and lead to deceptive experiences of life in general.

If people were re-educated in the use of themselves, the benefits in all areas of life would be tremendous. The "means" or the "how" of doing must be found in order to develop and maintain reliable sensory awareness. We should recognize that until new and correct experiences have been established, through the indirect process of inhibition and direction of the mind-body complex, it will be impossible to perform any new act satisfactorily. Recognizing this vital connection marks the point of departure between methods of teaching on a conscious basis and those on a subconscious basis. We must learn to inhibit our habitual reaction to the wish to perform an act—to refuse to "do" anything when a stimulus comes to us, until reason and judgment have entered in—and then give attention to the new, guiding, conscious directions to the organism, through the integrity of the head-neck-back relationship. These new directions are absolutely necessary for the improvement of our psycho-physical use in performing the act.

Let's take the example of writing, an everyday act. Most of us react to this stimulus by slumping over the paper, causing the neck to stiffen, the head to pull back and down into the shoulders, and the back to shorten and narrow and to twist to one side. We proceed further by leaning on one elbow, holding the head on one side, gripping the pen too tightly and stiffening the writing hand, arm, and shoulder. Many of us move the whole arm to write when it is only necessary to move the fingers. The feet are usually wrapped around each other under the chair, causing undue tension in the legs and lower back.

In contrast, the conscious coordinated means of writing can be carried out as follows. Place pen and paper on the desk (preferably on a sloping surface) and then inhibit your habitual reaction to them by refusing to proceed directly. Instead, think your neck free, your head forward and up, and your back to lengthen and widen. Keeping these directions as priority, place your feet easily on the floor, lean forward from your hip joints *without slumping*, place your left hand gently on the paper to steady it, and pick up the pen. Move the pen to the point where you will begin writing; but before actually writing, give again the mental directions to the head, neck, and back. Think also of freedom in your shoulder. Begin writing by moving only the fingers, not the whole arm and shoulder. This description is the coordinated means of performing the act of writing. Most of us, however, cannot do this successfully without the guidance of a teacher. Please note that constructive awareness cannot be imparted through the written or spoken word. It must be *experienced*.

Someone may say that "natural" athletes perform easily because they are conscious of what they are doing. But this is true only in relation to the *specific* skill that they have. In general, such athletes suffer from the same problem as the rest of us. They do not consciously control the use of themselves *as a whole*, not only during their performance, but also in the everyday acts of their lives. In other words, "natural" athletes can display that beautiful coordination in performing that we all love to see, but can be seen to revert to habitual, uncoordinated use in "normal" life.

Sensory Appreciation, Emotion, Memory

We can now consider another vital part of our make-up: the mysterious, unpredictable element in us known as emotion.

Emotion is intimately connected not only to our thoughts, but also to the excessive muscle tension caused by our misuse of the mind-body complex.

The basic sense of personal selfhood, the "I," could be termed a thought-emotion. It is the constant which inheres throughout all the vicissitudes of our lives, essentially unchanged and unchanging. This essential "I" is the core of one's intelligence, the root thought from which all other thoughts spring. Similarly, it is the root emotion from which all other emotions spring. Every thought, every memory and every emotion which one experiences is born within the ocean of this ego. This thought-emotion, this "I," is the personality.

All subsequent thought-emotions which grow from this root, however—from dark despair to beatific bliss—are subject to change. Because they must be expressed through the body, they will also be influenced by the quality of our use of the organism, as well as our sensory appreciation. We all know the feeling of being unable to freely express our emotions. The reason for this is excessive muscle tension due to misuse of the psycho-physical mechanisms, which brings fear, anxiety, hatred, and every other form of negative emotion. The condition of our muscles reveals our mental-emotional state. There is no negative thought-emotion which does not show up somewhere in the body as too much muscle tension. Equally, there is no positive thought-emotion which does not show up as a release of muscle tension. Does any thought exist independently of an accompanying emotion and muscular reaction?

If we are ever to prevent the pendulum of emotion from swinging fitfully and compulsively from blind bursts of hatred, the father of violence, to extremes of exaggerated ecstasy and "end-gaining" enthusiasm, then we must use our reasoning powers to improve our use of the self and subsequently our sensory appreciation. Doing so allows us to get rid of our negative emotions more easily and express our positive ones more freely.

In the individual's attempts to look deep within herself, and to do so impartially, it is painfully difficult to separate thoughts from emotions. That is, she is never certain whether or not she is being too emotional about a thought or too dryly intellectual about an emotion. The ability to strike a balance here is essential if she wishes to gain more self-knowledge and more self-control. This ability, therefore, is important to every spiritual seeker, because it is necessary to rise above such emotions such as are usually aroused in people through things like alcohol, drugs, faith-healing, and religious revivalism. These generally lead to nothing more than muddling through by instinct. People are always looking for a cure or relief from "life's hardships" outside themselves. The ability to make progressive change lies in our own minds when we look inside ourselves and learn reasoned, constructive awareness.

Let us now look to memory. Inefficient psycho-physical functioning will adversely affect our ability to register and remember impressions. Poor memory will, in turn, hinder our ability to reason, as reasoning depends upon the association of remembered facts. Our ability to assimilate and remember things depends upon the standard of our sensory appreciation, which is in turn determined by the quality of our psycho-physical use and functioning.

Nowadays an exaggerated value is placed on "intelligence" which manifests itself in a specific way, such as being able to remember an amazing number of facts about a particular subject. Assessment should be made, not only of the usefulness of the information remembered, but also of the person's *general* ability to be practical and lead a life of all-round usefulness in daily activities. To what avail is all this specific "knowledge" if satisfactory psycho-physical functioning is sacrificed in order to acquire it?

Sensory Appreciation and Happiness

Let us now consider sensory appreciation in relation to the presence or lack of that elusive condition we are all seeking, namely happiness. The reason for the lack of happiness in both

children and adults is, with few exceptions, a constantly deteriorating use of the mind-body complex. This deterioration can reach
such a deep level that it becomes a perverted condition akin to ill-
health that is in a strange way enjoyed.

A great deal of happiness, on the other hand, can be seen when
the child or adult is using the organism well, and therefore successfully, in any activity—be it simple or complicated. The vast
majority of us, however, need to re-learn how to use the organism
well. As we do so through the process of learning constructive
awareness, conscious fundamental psycho-physical experiences
are continuous; these connote real growth and development in all
acts of life. Establishing them is inseparable from that psycho-
physical-emotional-spiritual state which we call "happiness."

An example of a conscious fundamental psycho-physical experience is one such as that described earlier of the process of writing using the principles of constructive awareness. These
principles can be applied, not only to such acts as walking, sitting,
standing, eating, cleaning ourselves, bending, lifting, running,
and so on, but also to the whole range of human activity in all its
wonderful diversity.

The constantly deteriorating use of the mind-body complex can
reach a crucial stage where we are unable to experience anything
new, because boredom sets in and stultifies our potential to grow.
This is a tragedy of "old-age," when people retire from their usual
daily routine and cannot adapt to new conditions. Some other
people, thinking that at a certain age they have "grown up" and
"know" everything, decide there is therefore nothing more to
learn. Monotony and discontent are the results of this condition.

New experiences that bring a gradual improvement in our
psycho-physical use and functioning on a plane of constructive
awareness are essential. They allow us to command an increasingly high standard of functioning which makes for better health,
more happiness, and the opportunity to realize our potentialities.
A purely intellectual consideration of constructive awareness as
involved with this process will bring no real understanding and

can never equal the "Aha!" experience of it. Only the person who has such an experience can see that it points to a level of mind-body functioning almost unlimited in its possibilities.

New and unfamiliar ideas or experiences can only be satisfactorily conceived when the human being is in a state of co-ordinated activity, of psycho-physical unity. Co-ordination also brings a sound understanding of "cause and effect" in relation to the use of the mind-body complex and in relation to the problems of everyday life.

Sensory Appreciation, Mysticism, Science

This leads us on to a consideration of the mystic who is trying too hard to penetrate the deeper regions of mind in order to experience the Overself. By "too hard," I mean to the extent that the world, including the body, is dismissed as mere illusion. Because of this attitude to the body, she will be suffering from misuse of it which leads to excessive muscle tension and faulty sensory awareness. Any mystical experiences she may have during meditation will be affected by this imbalance between her mind and body.

These statements are made from the practical standpoint, but the philosophic one should be noted here as well. It says that the body is a part of the mind, a state of consciousness. If this huge area of the mind known as the body is constantly sending inaccurate reports to the self, then like the rest of us, everything the mystic has learned through scriptures, holy persons, gurus, and so on will be colored and influenced by these inaccurate sensory reports. Her excessive muscle tension, faulty sensory awareness, and garnered knowledge cause her to have certain propensities; cause her to *hold* (as muscle tension) certain beliefs. These beliefs, in turn, will affect her idea of what genuine mystical experience is.

The mystic must use reason and subject her experiences to rigorous analysis to determine if they are genuine divine revelations or fabrications of her own mind. Emotion, in addition, is an important factor in such cases. A highly-charged emotional state *during* her "vision" can also blind her to the real content and meaning of her ecstatic experience. With this improper balance of these aspects of her being, her ability to accurately convey the meaning of her experience to other people is also questionable. The value of a scientific attitude to mystical experience is immense.

The scientist, however, has a similar problem, but in reverse. Too often, she fails to understand that all the information she gleans from the "outside" world has to be experienced and assimilated ultimately by a psycho-physical mechanism which is out of balance due to her own misuse of it. This misuse causes her, like the mystic, to have excessive muscle tension and inaccurate sensory awareness—all combining to affect and color every piece of information that she accumulates. Whether she is looking through an electron microscope at the wonders of the subatomic world, or taking readings from a machine that registers data to the nth degree, this information has to be registered by an organism that functions inaccurately. In other words, relativity still reigns even in the subatomic world; since here also whatever is seen through the electron microscope can only be seen ultimately by her mind, via the eyes, it is not what it appears to be. No amount of "facts" about the "things" in the universe, microcosmic to macrocosmic, no accumulation of information, no matter how vast, will ever reveal its essence, *Mind*.

The scientist who looks constantly at the "outside" phenomena of the universe will search vainly for the hidden springs of life in ever-decreasing or increasing circles. But before she is in danger of disappearing into her own lab equipment, she could save much time and energy by combining the subjective, meditative path of the mystic with her healthy scientific rationality. Intellectual musing about the nature of reality cannot lead to, or be a substitute for, the direct experience of it. Such an experience must be of the highest.

It is a curious fact, for example, that a study of physiology and anatomy is considered to be an investigation of the "inside" of a human being, when it is, in actuality, a study of the inner workings of the body, including the brain. Such study of the body, brain, and nervous system tells us a great deal about these things. But it tells us nothing about that intangible subjectively discovered miracle which is our essence, namely, mind.

Every belief we hold about ourselves, every opinion that we have about any matter, every thought we think, and every act we carry out in our daily lives is influenced by the quality of our use of the mind-body complex and our sensory appreciation. If this quality is poor, then—whether we are inclined mystically or scientifically—we should hold open to question our beliefs, opinions, thoughts, and deeds.

If you want to enjoy inner peace, you must practice inner detachment.

Paul Brunton

9

DETACHMENT AND THE WAY
OF INSPIRED ACTION

IT IS trite but true that the whole stretch of each incarnation on this spinning globe, from rocking cradle to rolling hearse, is like a passing show, a mystery play that is over all too quickly and leaves us wondering what the plot was. It is even more trite but just as true that all the attachments we accrue, be they people or possessions, will be left behind when we finally arrive at that Great Transition into another form of consciousness that we curiously call death. How trivial must the travail of her past life seem to a dying woman! If at the end of it, we have not learned from life to detach ourselves from its vicissitudes, people, and possessions, then death will surely do it for us. It is the only certain event which will occur for all of us as a result of being born. This fact alone should be enough to convince us that a calm, inner detachment from the varied ups and downs of our lives is a worthwhile goal to achieve.

Such an achievement, alas! is far from easy. It is in fact among the most difficult of all to attain. How are we to become detached in our hearts from our loved ones, our precious possessions, our love of nature, of the arts or whatever? Such a state, it seems, can be achieved only by a true Sage or Master, while we lesser mortals can only aspire to it. This aspiration, however, can be enough to start us out on the road to attaining it. We can cultivate it a bit at a time as we gain more life experience and grow older and, hopefully, wiser.

To become free in both heart and mind, it is necessary to cultivate philosophic inner detachment—to shake off the common, habitual state of being conditioned and unbalanced. Freedom is a state of mind which can be achieved through learning how to be yourself no matter what your worldly circumstances may be. You can learn how to stay back from the demands of the frenzied, modern world, yet be fully involved in it. All events in your life will be seen as transient, recognized as comings and goings until they finally pass into death. Such events can be taken and experienced with a calm detachment.

With others, you can share in the pleasures and miseries of this planet. As you live and work you cultivate self-awareness and learn to stand back as a witness to all of it, mentally in control, the watcher as well as the participator.

If you truly achieve this self-awareness, you can even more easily cultivate the finer feelings of warm love, compassion, and altruism. You will not adopt an attitude of cold indifference like those who lose sight of the value of remaining practical in their spiritual endeavors and who denounce the world and everyone and everything in it as an illusion, people who do not realize that the Appearance is continuous with the Real. Neither will you be interested in the way of the ascetic who attempts to sever herself from the rest of the world, tries to live apart from its activities. You will realize that the true way is to foster your spiritual aspirations while you take an active part in worldly affairs.

The state of the true Sage is something for the aspirant to aim for. The Sage has reached that height where some part of her is always the untouched, impartial witness who sees things and events for what they really are. In your efforts to find peace, you will see that you cannot do so until you learn how to allow other people to find theirs in their own way. You can learn that what other people do and say is not your concern, because you have enough work to do on yourself in order to reach philosophic maturity.

Success or failure, right or wrong, as commonly judged by

human standards will not trouble the Sage's mind, will not disturb her inner poise, inner peace. She will maintain her equanimity whether life be full of hardships or pleasures. This poise will ensure that she does not experience those extreme moods which haunt an ultrasensitive person whose days are either darkened with dejection or lit up with exaggerated joy.

Cultivating such inner detachment will provide a continuous and excellent training in self-control, will lead to mental and emotional stability and a better knowledge of the self. You can learn the difficult art of living the spiritual life while, at the same time, balancing it with practical participation in worldly activities. Such a combination can lead to inner peace and seeing worldly life as the passing show that it really is. It will then be easier to take life philosophically.

It is essential here to stress the profundity, warmth, compassion, and altruism of real inner detachment which allows us, paradoxically, to be fully involved with the affairs of the world in an inspired way. Philosophic inner detachment must not be confused with cold lethargy, cold indifference. If the goal is to be worthy, it must not be bereft of loving feelings, must not be an icy one. Detachment does *not* mean losing interest in one's life, or in other people, or in worldly affairs.

The practices of altruism and cheerfulness must be cultivated to ensure that you do not lose the finer human feelings. Goodwill and good feeling must become part of your make-up; this will prevent you from becoming fanatical about calmness and detachment, prevent you from becoming cold and indifferent. You can attempt to light up the world with a wholehearted smile while, at the same time, reserving just a wee corner of that smile for yourself, as you adopt the position of the witness in the varied happenings of your life.

Balanced detachment should be the goal of the seeker. Don't step away from affectionate, intimate, human relationships. Normal human feelings, likes, and dislikes need not be lost. They can live and thrive side by side with inner renunciation.

The seeker who achieves balanced detachment will rise above the influence of other people who constantly suggest and advise her how to think and behave. She will be able to cope calmly with the pressures that they unwittingly put upon her; she will be content to mind her own business and leave others to theirs.

You may think that the achievement of this philosophic inner detachment is impossible; but given enough time, enough understanding, and enough work at it, it can be fulfilled. We must look to the Sage or the Master as an example to inspire us. We must not be daunted by the enormity of the task. If we feel that to reach such heights of complete detachment is beyond our capacities, then we will be faced with the gloomy prospect that just some wee bit of it will come by itself, through weariness and fatigue, when we are old dotards, when we could hardly claim even that little as our own conscious achievement. Would it not be better to cultivate it when we are yet young enough so that it becomes our own positive possession?

All of the foregoing principles about philosophic inner detachment set up an ideal, as stated earlier, for us to aspire to. Its achievement is the hallmark of the true Sage and its enormous difficulty must not be underrated. We would, however, be right in questioning whether total detachment from people and possessions is possible for anyone who has to deal with the world and the pressures of living. We must be careful to avoid searching after impossible goals, careful not to lose the finer feelings of love, humility, compassion, and altruism as we seek to free our hearts and strengthen our minds.

So let us finish this initial deliberation of philosophic inner detachment with a question that will lead us into a consideration of its relationship to constructive awareness. This question, which is often asked, is: "How is it possible to keep the mind in constant awareness of the inner life, when so often it has to give undeviating attention to the necessary acts of earning a living?"

The answer is, of course, that the mind must be trained, must be disciplined. "Yes," you declare, "but such a task seems impossible. Where am I to begin, if I am to become the master of my mind and achieve inner detachment?"

Perhaps this little story will help. Recently, a friend of mine said to me in utter frustration that try as he may, he was incapable of leading the kind of spiritual life that he fervently wished to live—that life which the Sages and Masters, past and present, have exhorted humankind to live. He was full of good intentions and enthusiasm, but something kept blocking him and frustrating his efforts to improve. I could see that he was very uptight because of deep muscular tension patterns that he had developed through misuse of his psycho-physical organism. So I suggested that perhaps it would be better not to set his sights too high. Perhaps he should first deal with his misuse to get rid of his excessive muscle tension. In other words, he could still continue his spiritual quest, but make a start by facing his most immediate problem—his psycho-physical condition that was the cause of his frustration.

In his case, he had little chance of achieving inner detachment, because he could not free himself from his habitual, harmful patterns of behavior that were causing the excessive muscle tension. He was truly their slave. This man had to learn detachment in a slightly, not completely, different sense.

But before going on with this story, let us return to the situation of a person being taught constructive awareness by a competent teacher. The principles of non end-gaining, of attending to the co-ordinated "means" of doing something, of inhibiting her habitual reaction of doing it in the old, familiar way, of not caring about whether the result of her doing is good or bad have all been explained to her. She understands intellectually what is required in order to perform the act in the new way. But, as soon as she moves, she resorts immediately to the old, habitual way. Why is this so? The reason is that the habit of trying to be right, which has been drummed into her since early childhood, dominates her way of being and doing. As a result, *she cannot remain detached enough, cannot take the position of the witness and remain impartial enough to allow the new co-ordinated "means" of performing the act to take place.* The new procedures are simply too difficult because they are not in keeping with her habitual use of the mind-body complex.

In my experience of teaching constructive awareness, I have met very few people who, in attempting to carry out a decision to make a given change, can keep that decision. In other words, few people can stay detached from their old, habitual, harmful patterns of use. Few people can stay detached from the fear and anxiety of "getting it right."

Inhibition is the key here. Even after it has been explained in detail to the pupil and she has practiced it a few times under the teacher's guidance, she will resort to the habitual way of doing as soon as the teacher stops reminding her.

For example, during the lesson there is a short period of time when the teacher talks the pupil through a procedure—say, standing up out of the chair. The teacher reminds her of what to think of in order to move in a co-ordinated way. When the pupil has reached the point of standing upright, the teacher then sneakily tests her by asking her to take a step forward. The pupil will do so immediately in her familiar way and neglect to inhibit her habitual reaction. The teacher points out that the reason for asking her to move her feet was to give her an opportunity to practice "inhibition" and "direction," and not to move until she had done so. The pupil replies that she forgot.

This is understandable. As we are dominated by subconscious, habitual behavior, the difficulty of remembering to inhibit or stop cannot be emphasized enough. The person who can learn the art of inhibition, who can consciously attend to the co-ordinated "means" of performing an act, who can truly stand back and witness herself, who can stop worrying about the result, good or bad, who can translate all this into practice will experience detachment in the basic sense. This detachment is not different from the philosophic inner detachment described earlier; it is a vital part of it. When you attempt the detachment required in learning constructive awareness, you will appreciate even more

the tremendous difficulty of achieving philosophic inner detachment. This is what happened with my friend who was suffering
from excessive muscle tension.

The secret is to remember, as often as possible, to observe
yourself, to be aware not only *what* you are thinking, feeling, saying, or doing, but *how* you are doing any task whatsoever. This
cultivation of self-awareness should become a constant in your
life and is one of the most valuable procedures on any kind of
spiritual path. This practice of constructive awareness provides a
continuous and excellent training in self-control that serves as a
basis for the self-control needed to cultivate philosophic inner
detachment. This practice will also bring the enjoyment of those
fruits such as mental equanimity, emotional stability, and a better
knowledge of the self. This is indeed a vital part of philosophic
self-control.

Can you see now how detachment through constructive awareness provides a large part of the answer to the question asked at
the end of the initial consideration of philosophic inner detachment? By means of inhibition and direction, the mind can be consciously and constantly engaged in the co-ordinated "means" of
performing an act. This constitutes a vital part of the constant
involvement of the mind in the inner life, while still giving attention—and quite often unswerving attention—to the necessary
tasks of earning a livelihood.

Constructive Awareness and Inspired Action

Let us go on to consider the relationship of inner detachment
to the way of inspired action. Apart from death, deep sleep is the
most profound form of detachment. For a third of our lives, we are
engaged in this almost non-activity where we remain totally
oblivious to the world and its cares, joys, and activities. During
deep sleep we are unaware of other people who may attempt con-
versation with us, or who may stealthily creep up on us with intentions of physical violence. The depth of our unawareness is so
great that we make no response. Similarly with things: Trains

clatter by on the bridge just above the house, or heavy motor traffic runs constantly past immediately outside the window. But if we have become used to such loud noises, we remain blissfully asleep.

How could we function adequately and healthily in the world without this blessed boon of sleep? It replenishes our tired selves every night, so that we can better cope with the world in the waking state. We are all aware that a lack of sleep leads to a devitalized state of weary activity during wakefulness. If we become over-attached to our business commitments, to the point of forcing ourselves to habitually go without sufficient sleep, then Nature will teach us a lesson in the form of illness via a nervous breakdown. Conversely, adequate sleep allows us to function well with energy and vitality in the waking state, and this makes us more happy and content. Our daily activities, our interactions with people, things, and events become more inspired because of this blessing of detached, deep sleep, this almost non-activity.

We know no peace in the waking state that can rival that which we experience in deep sleep. This is truly detachment which Nature imposes on us, whether we like it or not. As we move ever closer to the detachment of death, She constantly invites us to learn this art of detachment consciously.

In deep sleep, we are really at peace. But we are unaware of that at the time of its occurrence. Its lingering calm is often felt for a few moments just after the point of waking. But such is the demand made on us by the busy world, that calm is quickly lost and forgotten as we are swallowed up by our daily activities.

Meditation is an attempt to experience the peace of deep sleep *and be aware of it at the same time.* It is an attempt to achieve that fourth state of consciousness where one experiences the beatific peace of communion with the Overself—the state permanently attained by the Sage. The Sage who has come through the fires of hell to the achievement of spiritual and philosophical maturity goes through life with this constant awareness of the Overself as the background of all her activities, whether she be awake, asleep, or a-dream.

Through success in this kind of meditation, we will come to realize that inner detachment is the ally of inspired action. This is another of those great truths which invariably turn out to be paradoxical.

Alas! few of us have achieved the advanced state of the Master. We can only aspire to it and must struggle with attempts at inspired action during our trafficking with the world, and try to withdraw and become detached from it with intermittent spells of meditation. Repetition of such attempts is the key. Repetition brings conviction. The combination of repetition and aspiration brings realization.

The repeated practice of meditation, combined with continuous constructive awareness, will allow you to know yourself better, will bring you closer to mental and emotional equilibrium, so that calmness will prevail amid the frenetic activity of the world. A state of undisturbed repose is possible, no matter what you are thinking or doing.

You will understand that true spirituality is a way of life with a deeper outlook on the world. It is neither obscure speculation nor scientific supposition. You will also see that it is hazardous to separate the common, practical affairs of life from spirituality and that it is necessary to combine activity with contemplation. The golden mean can be found.

Using inspired action as a means of attaining spirituality in the mundane world is at least as valid as trying to find spirituality by retreating into a sect, organization, convent, or monastery and wearing some kind of uniform that distinguishes you from other people and announces your spiritual aspirations to the world. Many spiritual seekers prefer to strive for a wise balance where they can remain inconspicuous and combine spirituality with rock'n'roll! Life is large enough to include the clamor of crowds and the warm comfort of love, along with the chill of arduous self-denial.

You will realize that it is unnecessary to live with your head in the clouds. Most of human existence on this earth is mundane.

But strive to recognize the miracle in this mundaneness. Strive to apply philosophic principles to this mundane world. The balanced life can be obtained where spirituality is sought in meditation as well as in daily personal activity.

Just as it is a vital part of philosophic inner detachment, constructive awareness is a vital part of inspired action. Paying attention to the co-ordinated use of the psycho-physical mechanisms, through restoring the integrity of the head-neck-back relationship while carrying out our daily tasks, can only lead to an improvement in the quality and results of those tasks.

If we are compassionate and altruistic, the combination of constructive awareness, inner detachment, and inspired action will show us how to purge the ego of the killing principle and learn to love the world, including every form of life in it, on it, and above it. We will not care for the welfare only of other humans, but also of all life-forms, be they animal, vegetable, or mineral.

With the added, vital element of constructive awareness, we can combine calm inner detachment with the vitality and dynamism of compassionate, altruistic, inspired action. This is practical spirituality.

The next type of meditation is the analytic.
It may deal with personal experience, general
events, universal laws, the nature of man,
and the reality of soul, but always it seeks by
analysis and reflection to understand."

Paul Brunton

10

INSPIRED REASONING

BOOKS on Alexander Technique usually ally it with health and hygiene. My main purpose so far in this little book has been, in (hopefully refreshing!) contrast, to ally it with the spiritual quest.

"Alexander Technique?" you may ask. "What's that? And why have you taken so long to mention it?"

Alexander Technique is precisely the process that I have been struggling to explain throughout the book, and which I have chosen to call "constructive awareness." I have avoided the term "Alexander Technique" because of unfortunate associations that obscure its vital significance.

This process, this non-ism, was named after its discoverer, Frederick Matthias Alexander. That may not have been such a bright idea. At any rate, people who do not understand it now throw it into the mix of numerous alternative therapies and methods of bodywork which abound in this New Age. An alternative therapy it certainly is not. Nor is it "bodywork." It is a re-education in the use of the self, based on intelligent reasoning and inspired intellectual analysis.

F.M. Alexander (1869–1955) was an actor, born in Tasmania, who developed throat trouble at an early age. After realizing that the medical profession could not cure him, he decided that whatever was wrong with him must be something he was doing to himself. This led him to spend years of meticulous study of himself in the mirror. He studied not only how he used his vocal mechanisms, but also his whole psycho-physical organism.

He saw that no movement of a specific part of his body could be done in isolation. Each movement was a function of his whole being. He realized also that he was completely dominated by habitual, unreasoned use of himself. After many years of experimenting, he gradually freed himself of that tyranny. This was a remarkable achievement, because his habits of being and doing were the very things he had to use in his investigations, but were also the things he had to change. Eventually, he discovered that inhibition was the key to fundamental change. As stated in chapter four, we cannot bring about real, effective change in ourselves unless we learn to inhibit or stop our old unreasoned habits. Knowing how to stop is another of our great needs.

The remarkable thing about Alexander was that he discovered inhibition experientially—not with scientific machinery, but through acute reasoning, observation, and analysis. He called the process "constructive conscious control." As mentioned in chapter four, he made this discovery many years before medical science confirmed that inhibition is a vital part of the functioning of the nervous system.

Another remarkable point about Alexander: He realized from the outset that what he had discovered was not merely an epidemic of misuse in the civilized world, but a psychological turning point in human evolution. He constantly asserted that the time is long overdue for us to change from habitual, unreasoned behavior and become consciously controlled, balanced beings, guided by reason and accurate sensory appreciation. We must learn how to use constructively the wonderful potential of our conscious minds, how to *think* of functioning co-ordinatedly in the humdrum activity of our hectic modern lives. To learn this is not to adopt some kind of mechanical physical culture, but is truly a vital, creative mental process. Such conscious change would allow us to come into that most wanted of all states at the psycho-physical level, a sound body in a sound mind.

He saw the ability in us to develop *constructive conscious control* through inhibition and direction, as *man's supreme inheritance* in relation to *the use of the self*, which is a *universal constant in living*. The words in italic are the titles of the four books he wrote during his lifetime.

Alexander was a man of vision and his strongest plea was for the person that he called his most important client, the child. He founded a school where, as in any other school, the three R's were taught. But the first priority for the children in his school was to learn the co-ordinated "means" of doing anything, so that balanced psycho-physical development took place. The children were guided without being made to fear being wrong. He also had that rare ability to take the long view and see that our liberation lies in teaching the children, so that subsequent generations can emulate them and become conscious, reasoning beings.

Constructive Awareness and Health

A few words are in order here about constructive awareness in relation to health. Good health is the basis of human happiness. This means that any kind of spiritual quest must be accompanied by the pursuit of good health. When a person is ill, nothing seems more important than becoming well again. Illness hampers our spiritual aspirations in varying degrees, depending on the seriousness of the illness. Sometimes we are so ill that we are unable to give any attention to our spiritual aspirations at all.

From the long-range spiritual perspective, of course, we must bear in mind that both good health and bad health are temporary. In the course of a lifetime, every human being experiences the comfort of well-being, as well as the misery of suffering. Lessons of value are undoubtedly present in both conditions. Nonetheless, we hold that health is so great a blessing as we go about our work on ourselves, that we are wise to cultivate it.

The causes of suffering through ill-health take many forms. One such form is the ordinary karmic consequence of violating the natural laws of the body—for example, over-indulgence in alcohol, tobacco, drugs, poor-quality food, lack of sleep, and insufficient natural exercise. Another form is the deeper karma caused by actions not only in this life but in previous lives—such as ill-treatment of other human beings and animals, which includes the slaughter and consumption of the latter. This is part of the mystery which perplexes many people who do not understand why they are suffering.

An example of ordinary karma is the misery of a hangover after the "pleasure" of drinking too much the night before. If, however, the overindulgence in alcohol becomes chronic, then this ordinary karma has a more serious result: among other things, a diseased liver which eventually ceases to function. In the case of smoking it is, again among other things, lung cancer. There is no great mystery here. The person who breaks these natural laws and continues to indulge in some addiction, despite the danger to health, is not in touch with her reason. She is incapable of reasoned behavior in this respect. This is common knowledge.

There exists, however, an area of uncommon knowledge that is of deep karmic significance. It is the effect on our health of how we use the mind-body complex in everyday living. Uncoordinated use of the psycho-physical mechanisms causes muscle-tension patterns, which in turn cause all kinds of warped conditions in the body. These unnatural conditions prevent the vital organs, particularly in the torso, from functioning properly. The organs such as the heart, lungs, liver, stomach, etc., depend for their efficient working on the spine being at its optimal length. When it is, and when excessive muscle tension is released, there is enough room and appropriate abdominal pressure for healthy functioning.

Misuse of the psycho-physical mechanisms causes the spine to distort. The person becomes shorter in stature, a situation which deteriorates as one gets older and bad habits of posture and movement become ever more firmly entrenched in the organism. The shortening of the whole spine causes the chest to fall, the lumbar spine to collapse inward, the abdomen to protrude, and the breath to become shallow and inadequate, along with many other defects. The vital organs are then expected to function efficiently in cramped, over-pressurized conditions. This they cannot do.

An analogy may help. If I ask you to wear, continually, a harness slung round your neck, down the length of your torso and under the crotch and then tighten this harness so that your torso is harmfully and painfully shortened and hunched, you will surely refuse to do so. This is what we do, however, to our vital organs through misuse; and this for a whole lifetime. Such adverse conditions cause displacement of the body's different parts, lowered functioning and vitality, and a reduced ability to resist disease. It becomes essential then that these displaced parts, including the vital organs, be restored to their proper places. This can be done consciously through the indirect, holistic, re-educative process of constructive awareness. To regain normal health, co-ordinated use of the mind-body complex is imperative.

Another deep aspect of health is its relation to love. Many of us try to cultivate the finer feelings of love, compassion, kindness, and so on, for other people and yet miss the fact that the body is made up of billions of intelligent, *living* beings, existing in a microcosmic universe, who deserve as much consideration as our human neighbors. Our ability to love others is questionable when we consider how we ill-treat these living beings through overindulgence of any and every kind and through misuse of the mind-body complex. "Love your neighbor *as yourself*" cannot be fully realized unless real love and respect for ourselves is cultivated. This is our first duty.

I don't claim that the co-ordinated use of the psycho-physical organism is a *guarantee* for good health. Health depends also upon the individual's moral, ethical, and spiritual state, together with the karmic effects already mentioned. But good use of the mind-body complex will allow one to cope better with any kind of illness should it arise. Lest it appear, however, that these statements contradict what has been said about misuse as a fundamental reason for ill-health, let me again emphasize that co-ordinated use of the self remains the missing link for the vast majority of humanity. It is also the blind spot of most medical professionals, who would do well to avail themselves of this vital knowledge.

Summary

The truths inherent in constructive conscious control or constructive awareness, as I have chosen to name it, are not the truths of an individual named F.M. Alexander. They are universal truths of the psycho-physical self as it functions in the waking state during the numerous repetitive activities of everyday life. Alexander was simply driven by a need and by his creativity, based on intuition and reason, to discover them. In the present-day state of humanity, recognizing these truths is of the utmost importance. We simply will not survive if we continue to grope blindly in the dark, guided by those old, harmful, subconscious habits which we unthinkingly call instinct.

The experiences that Alexander went through to become a conscious, reasoning being throw light on how our sensory mechanisms can be improved. When they are so improved, they will provide a more valid criterion for the self-criticism essential to lasting progress on the spiritual quest. Those who use this process have the opportunity for continuous testing of their sensory observations and impressions, because they are constantly projecting conscious directions for new and improved use of the self. They are thus *obliged to go on being aware* whether or not they are reverting to habitual misuse. Through this guiding principle, they find the way to "think in activity" and to combine this process with new sensory observation of the use of the self.

As Alexander says at the close of his book, *The Use of the Self*: "If a technique which can be proved to do this for an individual were to be made the basis of an educational plan, so that the growing generation could acquire a more valid criterion for self-judgment than is now possible with the prevailing condition of sensory misdirection of use, might not this lead in time to the substitution of reasoning reactions for those instinctive reactions which are manifested as prejudice, racial and otherwise, herd instinct, undue "self-determination" and rivalry, etc., which as we all deplore, have so far brought to naught our efforts to realize goodwill to all people and peace on earth?"

Attention is the soul of thinking and the root of perception.

Paul Brunton

11

THE "PLACE" OF CONSTRUCTIVE AWARENESS

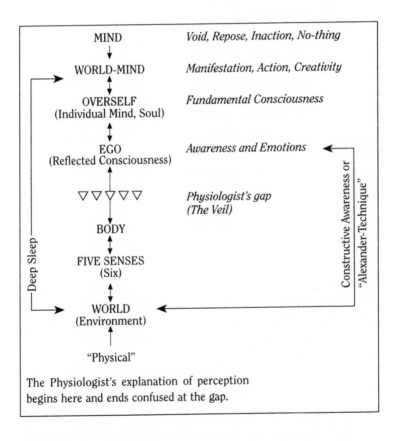

The Physiologist's explanation of perception
begins here and ends confused at the gap.

THE FIGURE above is an attempt to show the "place" of constructive awareness in the scheme of life. As with all such illustrations,

the value of this figure is limited. It is the power of the finite human   intellect to attain a true picture of such infinite things as Mind, World-Mind, and Overself.

Throughout this chapter, I will freely quote the ideas and paraphrase the words of philosopher Paul Brunton. The vocabulary he provides will be quite helpful to the purpose at hand. Not breaking up the flow of ideas with frequent references should greatly enhance readability. Appropriate references to sources appear at the end of the book.

Mind, placed at the top of the chart, is the source of all, the Great Void out of which the universe is made manifest. In Biblical terms it is "the darkness upon the face of the deep." It is "God-in-Repose," where there is complete inaction, where no-thing exists. It is eternal and free, beyond all the relativities of this world, beyond time and space, beyond human thought and human imagination. Mind is the invisible Absolute, the first and last Real, the Doer-Maker and Destroyer.

Placed beneath Mind is the World-Mind, which can be described as "Mind-in-Action." This is Mind in Its creative phase, from which all things in the universe—suns, worlds, human beings, etc.—are manifested. The universe is the World-Mind coming out of itself and making its manifestations out of its own substance (that is, Mind), just as the spider spins out a web from itself. In short, the universe is the imaginative construction of the World-Mind, which is God as Universal Intelligence and Creative Power. World-Mind is "God-in-Action," immanent in the world itself, the Lord of All, the God whom humans worship, yet cyclic in its existences.

Mind is the Real. Matter is the appearance it takes on. The universe comes by degrees out of the Ultimate Being, beyond which nothing is or could possibly be. Mind is measureless, with a Power equally measureless. World-Mind is this Power in operation, creating, maintaining, and in the end destroying what it has brought forth. Mind is the essence of the universe; the World-

Mind is manifestation. The only difference between these two is that essence is hidden and manifestation is known. It would, however, be a mistake to consider Mind as one entity and World-Mind as another separate from it. It is truer to consider World-Mind as the active function of Mind. Mind cannot be separated from its power; the two are one.

Next on the chart beneath World-Mind is the Overself. This is the essence or Soul of the individual human being, which is linked with, or rooted in, the Soul in the universe, the World-Mind. The individual not only exists within the World-Mind, he or she is born of it. The World-Mind reproduces something of itself in each individual entity we call the Soul or Overself. Overself is the fundamental consciousness of the individual. It shines through the ego but it is "apart" from the ego, for it stands in its own right and exists independently of the thoughts, emotions, etc., that constitute the ego. This consciousness is what enables human beings to act and think in the physical body. It is our diviner part. Blinded by the error of materialism, we identify it with the body.

The World-Mind originates our experience for us, but we ourselves mold it. It supplies the karmic-force material and we as individuals supply the space-time shape which this material takes. Thus there is a union of the individual with the universal.

The entire universe is but a thought in the World-Mind. Every object and every creature is simultaneously included in this thought, therefore every human being too. Through this relationship it is possible for an individual to attain some kind of union with IT. This should be the aim of any spiritual quest. The World-Mind operates through each person's consciousness as that person's Overself—something which is deeper than our ordinary thoughts and feelings, something that is our inmost, essential Self or Soul. If we can lift our awareness to the level of the Overself, we may meet in fellowship with the Divine. Through it, the World-Mind reveals something of its own mysterious nature. Ordinarily, we cannot directly penetrate that layer of mind that is continuous with and contiguous to the Overself. But during the deepest state of meditation, we may do so and thus realize that, through the Overself, we are indissolubly linked with the World-Mind.

The element in your consciousness which enables you to understand that you exist, which causes you to pronounce the words "I Am," is this spiritual element, here called Overself. It is really your basic self. The three activities of thinking, feeling, and willing are derived from it, are attributes and functions which belong to it. But our ordinary thinking, feeling, and acting do not express the Overself, for they are under the control of a different entity, the personal ego, which is the next step down the chart.

What is the ego but the Overself surrounded with barriers, conditioned by its instruments—the body, the feelings and the intellect—and forgetful of its own nature? This personal ego is put forth by the Overself. It has a reflected consciousness and derives its own light and power from the Overself, but imagines that it has its own original, and not derived, awareness.

The ego is a passing thing, but its source is not. For the "I" of the ego is supported by the "I" of the spiritual being, the spiritual self. Indeed the first derives its reality from the second and the second survives when the first passes away. But the ego must be there, for it is needed to be active in this world. At the center of human individuality lies the ego, the "I," the conscious thinker behind and beneath our everyday thoughts and acts, feelings and passions.

The ego's connection to the last stage on the chart, namely the so-called physical world, must also be considered. The body and the world are really, from the philosophic standpoint, one and the same. We will look at this in relation to the question of the "materiality" of the world and the body, and the "mentalness" of the ego, the individual mind.

At the bottom of the chart, an arrow points from the physical world to the senses, from the senses to the body, and from the body to the ego. Between the body and the ego is a zig-zag line representing the "physiologist's gap," the explanation of which is as follows.

The physiologist's explanation of how the individual mind perceives the world runs like this. The brain experiences the world through the senses of sight, hearing, touch, taste, and smell. When stimulated by some outside material object these senses cause physical sensations in the body, which are first conducted along the nerves to the brain and then taken up by the brain and converted into thought or mental perception. Scientists readily admit, however, that they still do not understand the process by which these sensations are converted into thought or perception. This step they don't understand is what mentalists call the "gap."

This "scientific" explanation truly puts the cart before the horse. It would truly make mind a product of matter. But people who hold a materialistic view of the world are walking around believing in a theory that has yet to be proved. The theory in fact offers no explanation at all, because it cannot cross the gap between unconscious mundane materiality and miraculous mentalness, mysterious consciousness. This gap is "The Veil" which the materialist cannot pierce. Mentalism reformulates the mystery as follows.

Proceeding downwards from the top of the chart, we see that the whole of this vast universe is a mental creation, the essence of which is Mind. From this Mind springs the World-Mind as Mind-in-action. Stars, suns, worlds, etc., are produced by the Creative Thought of the World-Mind. So too are human individuals who are also mental beings blessed with creativity. The Overself is the link between the World-Mind and the individual. Thus we move from Mind (Void, No-thing, Repose) to World-Mind (Creativity, Action) to Overself (Fundamental individual consciousness) to ego (Reflected consciousness).

With the Overself as its essence, the individual is constantly giving attention from its own center to the world. Attentiveness is a manifestation of the essence of humankind, of that Soul which stands higher than intellect, feeling, and body. Mentalism explains that we do not experience a world which is "out there." We experience only our own *perception* of the world, which is obviously *within* our consciousness. Our perception of the world IS what we call the world.

Constantly giving attention from its center outwards, the individual mind expands from this center. It is what is truly "out there" as far as our eyes can see, as far as our ears can hear, as far as our fingertips can reach, as richly as our tongues can taste, as pungently as our noses can smell and, just as importantly, as far as our creative imagination can stretch. What is the individual mind? It is that in us which is aware, which thinks, and which knows.

Whatever stimulus comes into the individual's field of awareness is strictly a matter of attention. The thought of a thing invariably *follows* attention to a thing; but the almost instantaneous rapidity with which it does so, together with the momentary character of both, produces the illusion of a single conscious act and we remain ignorant of the succession. Such is the magic of the mind whose incredible celerity of perception has been built up slowly over millions of years and thousands of lifetimes of relentless repetition of the act of giving attention to the world.

As can be seen from the chart, this level of "attending to the world" is the realm of constructive awareness. This is the realm of the ego, the individual mind, as it interacts through the mediums of the body and the senses with the world. The quality of this interaction, as stated in chapter eight, directly depends upon the effectiveness and accuracy of our sensory appreciation, which is, in turn, dependent upon the quality of our use of the mind-body complex. It makes perfect sense, then, to allow this so-called "physical" body to act and function optimally so that we may experience more accurately, and form a truer picture of, the world-thought of which we ourselves are parts. This is the vital task which must precede, or at least be carried out at the same time as, our spiritual and philosophical studies.

As stated earlier, the ego is the center of human individuality, the "I" which is the conscious thinker, individual mind. Constructive awareness is a function of this mind and is, therefore, a mental process. It has nothing to do with any kind of physical discipline or regime.

Two more parts of the diagram remain to be explained. Firstly, a connection can be seen from the World-Mind to the "physical" world along the line of deep sleep. Another connection exists from the ego to the world via the body and the senses. This indicates that the World-Mind is constantly projecting its idea, its creation, namely the world, whereas the ego is intermittently absorbed, between waking states, by the Overself during deep sleep (and obviously knows nothing of the world, including the body, at this time). It becomes aware of the world again on awakening as it is projected by the Overself and resumes its conscious interaction with the world via the body and the senses. This is meant to show that in the waking state, the individual mind makes its own world of experience; but it does not make it by itself, for behind it is the World-Mind which imposes its idea, the world, on all of us as individuals. The Infinite Mind is centered within its finited expression, the human ego. This is why we experience the same world, common to us all, as the idea projected by the World-Mind.

The second and last part to be explained is the double direction of the arrows from one state to another. For example, the Overself is connected to the World-Mind in one direction and to the ego in the other. Thus it is the Soul which constitutes the link between the human and the Divine.

Peace to all who peruse these pages
and to those who do not.

EPILOGUE

THE inspiration for this book is mainly from three sources: 1) the writings and teachings of Paul Brunton; 2) the writings and teachings of F.M. Alexander; 3) my own life experience. I wish to acknowledge these two men who have been such a profound influence on my life and thought.

Some details of F.M. Alexander have already been given in chapter ten, so this space will be devoted to information about Paul Brunton.

Every now and then a true spiritual light shines in this world in the form of a veritable Sage. Paul Brunton is such a Sage, and is also a man who did a great work in bringing Eastern philosophy to the West. To say just this would be to do him a grave injustice, because he not only brought these ancient teachings to the Occident; he also presented them in a way that the man or woman in the street can understand. He synthesized ancient Eastern and modern Western philosophy in a uniquely creative way. His teachings became a new, modern philosophy, not any kind of revivified corpse.

P.B., as he is affectionately known by readers of his many books, was born in England in 1898 and passed over in Switzerland in 1981.

Paul Brunton's profound humility and wisdom are apparent in his books. They and are also emphasized by the fact that, throughout his life, he repeatedly refused to accept any attempts by people to make him into a guru. He refused anyone who wished to be a follower and said that each of us must become our own guru.

He was a prolific writer. Ten books published during his lifetime have been read throughout the world. A further sixteen-volume *Notebooks* series was published posthumously. The titles of all his books are listed below.

Early Works of Paul Brunton:

A Search in Secret India

The Secret Path

A Search in Secret Egypt

A Message from Arunachala

A Hermit in the Himalayas

The Quest of the Overself

Discover Yourself (originally *The Inner Reality*)

The Hidden Teaching Beyond Yoga

The Wisdom of the Overself

The Spiritual Crisis of Man

Essays on the Quest (early writings published posthumously)

All the above are published by Rider & Co, London, and Samuel Weiser, Inc., York Beach, Maine (USA).

The following *Notebooks of Paul Brunton* consist of more than 7,000 pages of notes withheld by him for posthumous publication. They are part of a large work which he spoke of as his "Summing Up." There are sixteen volumes covering twenty-eight categories such as "The Quest," "From Birth to Rebirth," "The Reign of Relativity," "What is Philosophy?" "Mentalism," "World-Mind in Individual Mind," etc., all of which are of deep significance to any spiritual seeker. The *Notebooks* are published by Larson Publications for the Paul Brunton Philosophic Foundation in Burdett (near Ithaca), New York.

Volume 1: Perspectives. This volume is a representative survey
with sample chapters on each of the twenty-eight major topics
(categories) in the *Notebooks* series. Subsequent volumes
focus in depth on one to four categories.

Volume 2: The Quest

Volume 3: Practices For The Quest
           Relax and Retreat

Volume 4, Part 1: Meditation
           Part 2: The Body

Volume 5: Emotions and Ethics
           The Intellect

Volume 6: The Ego
           From Birth to Rebirth

Volume 7: Healing of the Self
           The Negatives

Volume 8: Reflections

Volume 9: Human Experience
           The Arts in Culture

Volume 10: The Orient

Volume 11: The Sensitives

Volume 12: The Religious Urge
           Reverential Life

Volume 13: Relativity, Philosophy, and Mind

Volume 14: Inspiration and the Overself

Volume 15: Advanced Contemplation
           The Peace within You

Volume 16: Enlightened Mind, Divine Mind

Further information on Paul Brunton's work can be obtained from:

The Paul Brunton Philosophic Foundation
Larson Publications
4936 Route 414
Burdett, New York 14818
U.S.A.

Further information on the Alexander Technique can be obtained from:

The Society of Teachers of the Alexander Technique
20 London House
266 Fulham Rd
London SW10 9EL
Great Britain

I am a teacher of the Alexander Technique and director of a training course for teachers at the

Ausbildungszentrum für F.M. Alexander Technik
Borstellstrasse 42
12167 Berlin
Germany

QUOTATIONS

List of Quotes from Paul Brunton's Works Used in this Text

Introduction Epigraph.
What philosophy seeks—and what most "systems" do not . . .: *Notebooks*, Vol. 13, pt. 2, ch. 3, no. 448.

Chapter 1, Epigraph 1.
With most people the reaction to . . .: *Notebooks*, Vol. 5, pt. 1, ch. 1, no. 294.

Chapter 3, Epigraph.
The faulty use of the body . . .: *Notebooks*, Vol. 4, pt. 2, ch. 2, no. 23.

Chapter 4, Epigraph.
The intelligence in the deeper human mind . . .: *Notebooks*, Vol. 13, pt. 3, ch. 1, no. 64.

Chapter 4, page 35:
"What is the path?" . . .: *Notebooks*, Vol. 9, pt. 1, ch. 2, no. 190.

Chapter 5, Epigraph.
It is in the joining of . . .: *The Quest of the Overself*, p. 76.

Chapter 6, Epigraph.
Consciousness of the Spirit . . .: *Notebooks*, Vol. 4, pt. 2, ch. 5, no. 111.
It is better, for instance . . .: *Notebooks*, Vol. 4, pt. 2, ch. 2, no. 13.

Chapter 7, Epigraph.
If the hatha yogis are right . . .: *Notebooks*, Vol. 4, pt. 2, ch. 6, no. 8.

Chapter 8, Epigraph.
Man's success in using his knowledge . . .: *Notebooks*, Vol. 7, pt. 2, ch. 3, no. 101.

Chapter 9, Epigraph.
If you want to enjoy inner peace . . .: *Notebooks*, Vol. 15, pt. 2, ch. 3, no. 91.

Chapter 10, Epigraph.
The next type of meditation . . .: *Notebooks*, Vol. 4, pt. 1, ch. 4, no. 1.

Chapter 11, Epigraph.
Attention is the soul of thinking and the root of perception.: *The Quest of the Overself*, p. 79.

The following quotes by Paul Brunton accompany the chapter eleven text as further reference material.

. . . Mind is the source of all . . . : *Notebooks*, Vol. 16, pt. 3, ch. 3, no. 56.

. . . God in Repose is Mind.: *Notebooks*, Vol. 16, pt. 3, ch. 3, no. 61.

As Mind, it is beyond all the relativities of this world, beyond time and space, human thought and human imagination. As World-Mind it is immanent in the world itself, the Lord of the All, the God whom men worship, yet cyclic in Its existences.: *Notebooks*, Vol. 16, pt. 3, ch. 3, no. 58.

Mind is the Real; matter is the appearance it takes on. The universe comes by degrees out of the Ultimate Being, beyond which nothing is or could possibly be. It is Mind, measureless, with a Power equally measureless. World-Mind is this Power in operation, creating, maintaining, and in the end destroying what it has brought forth.: *Notebooks*, Vol. 16, pt. 3, ch. 3, no. 68.

Mind is the first and last Real, the Doer-Maker and Destroyer. . . .: *Notebooks*, Vol. 16, pt. 3, ch. 3, no. 12.

The universe is the World-Mind coming out of itself and therefore making its manifestation out of its own substance—that is, Mind—just as the spider spins out a web from itself.: *Notebooks*, Vol. 16, pt. 3, ch. 3, no. 12.

The universe is the imaginative construction of the World-Mind.: *Notebooks*, Vol. 16, pt. 3, ch. 3, no. 14.

The World-Mind is God as universal intelligence and creative power.: *Notebooks*, Vol. 16, pt. 3, ch. 2, no 8.

. . . Between essence and manifestation the only difference is that essence is hidden and manifestation is known. . . .: *Notebooks*, Vol. 16, pt. 3, ch. 3, no. 65.

It would, however, be a mistake to consider the World-Mind as one entity and Mind as another separate from it. It would be truer to consider

World-Mind as the active function of Mind. Mind cannot be separated from its powers. The two are one. . . .: *Notebooks*, Vol. 16, pt. 3, ch. 3, no. 65.

The individual not only exists within the World-Mind, it is born *of* the World-Mind.: *Notebooks*, Vol. 16, pt. 1, ch. 1, no. 4.

The World-Mind reproduces something of itself in each individual entity we call the Soul, or Overself.: *Notebooks*, Vol. 16, pt. 1, ch. 1, no. 10.

. . . It [the Overself] is apart from the ego, for it stands in its own right and exists as an entity by itself. It is this consciousness which enables a man to act and think in the physical body and it is his diviner part. Blinded by the error of materialism, we identify it with the body itself.: *Notebooks*, Vol. 16, pt. 1, ch. 1, no. 16.

Thus the World-Mind originates our experience for us, but we ourselves mold it. It supplies the karmic-forces material and we as individuals supply the space-time shape which the material takes. Thus there is a union of the individual with the universal.: *Notebooks*, Vol. 16, pt. 1, ch. 1, no. 20.

This entire universe is but a thought in the Universal [World] Mind. Every object and every creature is simultaneously included in this thought; therefore every human being too. Through this relationship it is possible for a man to attain some kind of union with IT.: *Notebooks*, Vol. 16, pt. 1, ch. 1, no. 21.

There is something deeper than our ordinary thoughts and feelings, something that is our inmost essential self. It is the soul. It is here, if we can reach to it, that we may meet in fellowship with the Divine. Through it the World-Mind reveals something of its own mysterious nature.: *Notebooks*, Vol. 16, pt. 1, ch. 1, no. 37.

Ordinarily man cannot directly penetrate that layer of the mind which is continuous with, and contiguous to, the Overself. But during the deepest state of meditation, he may do so.: *Notebooks*, Vol. 16, pt. 1, ch. 1, no. 35.

That element in his consciousness which enables him to understand that he exists, which causes him to pronounce the words "I Am," is the spiritual element, here called Overself. It is really his basic self for the three activities of thinking feeling and willing are derived from it, are ripples spreading out of it, are attributes and functions which belong to it. But as we ordinarily think, feel and act, these activities do not express the Overself for they are under the control of a different entity, the personal ego.: *Notebooks*, Vol. 6, pt. 1, ch. 1, no. 1.

What is the ego but the Overself surrounded with barriers, conditioned by its instruments—the body, the feelings and the intellect—and forgetful of its own nature?: *Notebooks*, Vol. 6, pt. 1, ch. 1, no. 6.

The personal ego derives its own light of consciousness and power of activity from the Overself.: *Notebooks*, Vol. 6, pt. 1, ch. 1, no. 23.

The ego is put forth by the Overself.: *Notebooks*, Vol. 6, pt. 1, ch. 1, no. 24.

The ego is a passing thing, but its source is not.: *Notebooks*, Vol. 6, pt. 1, ch. 1, no. 29.

The Overself-consciousness is reflected into the ego, which then imagines that it has its own original, and not derived awareness.: *Notebooks*, Vol. 6, pt. 1, ch. 1, no. 33.

The ego must be there, for it is needed to be active in this world . . .: *Notebooks*, Vol. 6, pt. 1, ch. 1, no. 39.

The "I" of the ego is supported by the "I" of the spiritual being, the spiritual self. Indeed, the first derives its reality from the second and the second survives when the first passes away.: *Notebooks*, Vol. 6, pt. 1, ch. 1, no. 142.

The conscious thinker, the "I," the ego.: *Notebooks*, Vol. 6, pt. 1, ch. 1, no. 153.

One's ego, oneself, "I," lies behind and beneath thoughts and acts, feelings and passions.: *Notebooks*, Vol. 6, pt. 1, ch. 1, no. 154.

What is Mind? It is that in us which thinks, which is aware, and which knows.: *Notebooks*, Vol. 13, pt. 3, ch. 2, no. 128.

The thought of a thing invariably *follows* attention to a thing, but the almost instantaneous rapidity with which it does so, together with the momentary character of both, produces the illusion of a single conscious act, and we remain ignorant of the succession.: *Notebooks*, Vol. 13, pt. 3, ch. 2, no. 16.

Attentiveness, indeed, is a manifestation of the essence of man, of that soul which stands higher than intellect, feeling and body.: *The Quest of the Overself*, p. 79.

The Infinite Mind is centred within its finited expression, the human ego.: *Notebooks*, Vol. 16, pt. 1, ch. 1, no. 12.